We hope
life style
to live
God Bless
Jack

John 3:16

Please excuse
the mistakes as
Jacks secretary of 12 yrs.
has moved to Heaven!
But we know you
will enjoy the stories!
Thank you,
Marilyn
Prov. 3:6

So You Wanna Be a Cowboy?

True Events in the Lives of
Jack and Marilyn Kirby

By:

Jack Kirby

WestBow
PRESS
A DIVISION OF THOMAS NELSON

Copyright © 2012 Jack Kirby

All rights reserved. No part of this book may be used or reproduced by any means, graphic, electronic, or mechanical, including photocopying, recording, taping or by any information storage retrieval system without the written permission of the publisher except in the case of brief quotations embodied in critical articles and reviews.

WestBow Press books may be ordered through booksellers or by contacting:

WestBow Press
A Division of Thomas Nelson
1663 Liberty Drive
Bloomington, IN 47403
www.westbowpress.com
1-(866) 928-1240

Because of the dynamic nature of the Internet, any web addresses or links contained in this book may have changed since publication and may no longer be valid. The views expressed in this work are solely those of the author and do not necessarily reflect the views of the publisher, and the publisher hereby disclaims any responsibility for them.

Any people depicted in stock imagery provided by Thinkstock are models, and such images are being used for illustrative purposes only.

Certain stock imagery © Thinkstock.

ISBN: 978-1-4497-3653-8 (e)
ISBN: 978-1-4497-3654-5 (sc)
ISBN: 978-1-4497-3655-2 (hc)

Library of Congress Control Number: 2012900311

Printed in the United States of America

WestBow Press rev. date: 3/27/2012

Thoughts About the Authors and *So You Wanna Be a Cowboy?*

You've heard about people who have lived interesting lives…and just when you think you have heard it all, along come Jack and Marilyn Kirby. They have done more in their lifetimes than most people dream of. I have known them for over 65 years, and they have tales to tell. The best part is that their stories are all true!

—Doug Harvey,
2010 National Baseball Hall of Famer and
Retired National League Umpire

Jack Kirby built an American dream on a handshake founded in honor and integrity and guided by his rock-solid faith in God and all things good. Jack's successful business provided him with the resources to retire at 37 years old and then commit to a second career to fulfill his personal lifelong dream as a Cowboy. When he finally hung up this spurs, Jack hung his hat in a quiet, warm and loving home with his wife Marilyn at the Broken Spoke Golf Course and Resort in El Centro, California. "The Spoke," is another of wonderfully successful venture that Jack built. Jack's book gives us a unique peek at an America not seen in our modern day media. It's the America of Jefferson, Washington, Daniel Boone, Charlie Russell, Roy Rogers, John Wayne, and every average guy next door who had a dream and worked to capture it. [The book] is a great read, about horses, cows, big wrecks, trail drives, cowboys and cowgirls and the American dream. Be ready to fall on the floor slapping your sides with tears in your eyes on one page and bawling like a new born calf on the next. It will bring quiet smiles and the big guffaws will boil up uncontrollably. It is truly an American tale of success you will thoroughly enjoy.

—Bob Candland,
Former Publisher/Owner of the Tombstone
Tumbleweed Newspaper in Tombstone, Arizona
and United States History Teacher

Jack Kirby, with his varied background, is a master storyteller. He draws on his experiences to relate his fascinating stories to us in his folksy manner. With his reputation in the Imperial Valley of California as a businessman and restaurateur, people are surprised to hear that he is also an experienced cowboy and teamster. His colorful stories give the reader a taste of what the Old West has become.

—Robert Duncan

It was my pleasure to have pastured 10 years in El Centro, California. During those years, I was able to experience some of the cowboy way of life. I never enjoyed anything so much as saddling up my horse and going on a cattle drive with the Kirby's, Taylor's, and other Christian cowboys and cowgirls. When we would arrive at the field with cattle that we were going to move, I would start wondering what was going to happen to us today on the drive. Then we would all go to lunch together, and we would enjoy each others' stories of the day's events. Yes, 10 wonderful years of my life that will never be forgotten.

—Roy Smith, Member of "The Crew" and Former Pastor

I always enjoy seeing Jack and Marilyn Kirby because we always have a good laugh. Their great attributes are a genuine interest in people and an excellent sense of humor. It's what has kept them young and enthusiastic enjoyers of life. The world needs more people like Jack and Marilyn Kirby.

—Mark Russel,
Vice President of Rules and Competition for the P.G.A. Tour

I've been lucky the last ten years to be included in a group of friends who meet for coffee and nonsense every Sunday morning at our golf course. A local legend, Jack Kirby, is the senior member of our group and frequently directs the conversation by instigating the subject of the day's subject or debate. As a retired judicial officer, I'm often the target of Jack's dissatisfaction with our justice system, and I find myself required to defend decisions made by judges across the country that run contrary to Jack's frontier justice philosophy. Of course, I found his attitude to be a little different the day he was a defendant in my traffic court.

Along with solving all of the world's problems, we also hear a lot of stories from our group. Jack has had more experiences than any of us and hearing about his life as a cowboy, businessman, restaurateur, golf course developer, and civic leader has been fascinating. Stories about his famous Clydesdales, Tom and Jerry, are particularly fun to hear, and I've heard what seems like an unending supply of these tales.

Naturally, I was delighted when Jack announced he was going to compile some of his stories and get them published. Jack has been fortunate to lead a full and rich life, and we are fortunate to share some of his experiences through his book.

—F. King Kimball,
Retired Superior Court Commissioner

Jack Kirby is a great friend and I am so grateful I got to know him more on a personal level these past few years. He asked that I keep this memoir short and sweet, so I'll try and honor his request.

Jack is a graduate of the great Central Union High School and he has taken much pride in his school. Jack has always been a strong supporter of all the activities connected with Central Union, but I know his passion is football. While I was a player in the 60's, Jack was the man "behind the scenes" making sure our teams were well taken care of. I can remember later on as a coach when the teams would go downtown to the Cameo restaurant that Jack owned and operated, and we had a tremendous pre-game meal with all the trimmings! In more recent times, Jack suggested that our football team run onto the field behind a Spartan on a horse to get the players, coaches, and fans all fired up! Boy, did that ever catch on and now our community has taken ownership of this new tradition that Jack Kirby made happen. Every Spartan fan asks about that horse and now when teams come to Central, they know about "that Horse!" Jack also had his "Clydesdales" that would perform in the Christmas parade and other events in and out of the Valley. Jack sure looked like a "Happy Cowboy" when he was with those horses!

I would sincerely like to thank Jack, Marilyn, and his family for being such an important part of what has made Central Union High the school that it is today—a school filled with pride, tradition and honor. Thank you Jack for being a friend and you are most definitely a TRUE-BLUE SPARTAN!

—Steve Evangelist,
Assistant Principal of Athletics at Central Union High School

In 1965, we accepted a call to the El Centro Church of the Nazarene as their pastor where we met the Kirby family. We became instant friends. Their book is about cattle drives. I was fortunate to go on a few and to ride a horse on the drag with Marilyn and Vera, of course. I would sing to the steers, "Come on boys! Jesus loves you this I know," to encourage them to keep up. The other hands would laugh at my singing to the steers. I really loved those experiences. So much fun! I know you will enjoy their stories.

—Gwen (McGuire) Wright,
Former Travel Secretary to the General Superintendents of the Church of the Nazarene

When I was 10 years old, my father took me golfing for the first time. I soon found myself looking down the #1 fairway at Broken Spoke not knowing what to expect. The game was new and abstract to me, similar to a kid trying to tie his shoe for the first time. I hit a club (which I later learned was a 3 wood) 100 yards down the fairway and remember my father giving me an "Atta Boy!" Although this shot was my 1st shot ever as a golfer, I soon learned (after 10 balls) that it would be my only good shot of the day. As I envisioned this drive over and over in my mind for the next few days, I again asked my father to take me back out Broken Spoke. From that point forward, I was hooked on the sport.

My home course as a kid would have never been a reality without the efforts from Mr. and Mrs. Jack Kirby. Later on in my life would I soon recognize how the contributions of the Kirby's would soon impact not only my outlook on golf, but other young golfers in years to come. As a current high school golf coach, I find my golfers learning in the same manner and scenarios as I did as a kid on the very same course, Broken Spoke. More astounding, the same efforts in youth golf are still in place as they were 25 years ago. In the current day, it is evident that kids, teenagers, and adults are showing how much a local golf course can impact one's life through recreation and competition.

The Kirby family is to be recognized for their endless efforts in the development of our local golf community for over 25 years. When the idea came about in the 1980's to build a golf course in the heart of El Centro, the Kirby family sure did "Hit it on the nose!"

I speak for the youth of today and in the future…Jack and Marilyn, thank you!

—A.J. Escalera,
Boys Golf Coach and Teacher at Southwest High School

MARILYN AND I DEDICATE THIS BOOK TO OUR CHILDREN, GRANDCHILDREN, AND GREAT GRANDCHILDREN.

Paul and Terri Kirby
Their Children: Katie, husband Jordan, and Bobby

Wes and Caroline Kirby
Their Children: Nicole, Amber, and Amber's daughter Abygail

Robin and Michael Martin
Their Children: Cheryl, Jeff, Taryn, Marilyn, and Taylor

Cheryl and Victor Pitones
Their Children: Zachary, wife Melissa, Alexandra, and Victoria

Jeff and Julissa Martin
Their Children: Angela and ReAnne

My Sister: Norma Richard

These are seven of our nine grandchildren.

Contents

Preface   *xv*
Acknowledgements   *xvii*

PART 1   **xix**

1. Slowly Becoming a Cowboy   1
2. First Meeting with My Best Friend   4
3. My First Cattle Drive   5
4. My First Roped Steer   6
5. Most Moves Were Fun and Easy   8
6. How We Moved From Field to Field   10
7. 200 Head of Our Own   13
8. Gifts for Mexico   15
9. Practice Roping in Arenas   17
10. Michael's Invention for Moving Cattle   23
11. Lost Antique   25
12. Stampede from Heber to El Centro   27
13. Twelve Mile Move   31
14. Move from Hartman Williams Feed Lot   34
15. Another Move Down Highway 98   36
16. Haythorn Ranch: Ogallala, Nebraska   38

17. Rainstorm on Highway 111	40
18. New Calves on Sudan Grass	42
19. Marilyn's Rodeos	47
20. Sugar Beets Pasture	51
21. We Took No Pictures	53
22. The Loss of Our Friends	55
23. The Lettuce Patch	57
24. A Wild West Lunch	59
25. A Steer Guest for Dinner	60
26. Lost and Found Horses	62
27. Tom and Jerry Save the Day	64
28. The Different Cattle That We Received	66
29. The Last Cattle Drive	68
PART 2	**71**
30. After 25 Years of Cattle Drives	73
31. The Trip of a Lifetime	75
32. We Found Our Hitch	78
33. Waverly, Iowa Auction	82
34. Our Three-Seated Surrey	85
35. Different Jobs for Tom and Jerry	87
36. Cheyenne Days	95
37. Cheyenne Parade Wrecks	102
38. Bill Coors and a New Harness	104

39. Celebrities	107
40. Weddings and Goodbyes	115
41. Fair Time	119
42. A Tribute to My Friend	122
43. Two New Tom and Jerry's	126
44. Kirbyland U.S.A.	131
45. Marilyn's Duck Named Dugan	137
46. Molly and Friends	140
47. The P.G.A. Tour	143
48. Hudson and Waterloo, Iowa	147
49. Helping Tim Kirby	151
50. Knotts Berry Farm	153
51. Buffalo, Oklahoma	158
52. Tragedy with Kaz	164
53. Our Family Ski Trips	167
54. Sailing the West Indies	169
55. Flying: Another New Experience	171
56. Mexico City Olympics	173
57. Nebraska: My Home State	177
Afterword	*181*
Appendix	*183*

Preface

Ever since I can remember, I've always been a go-getter. If I wanted to do something, I went out and did it. In 1949, after I graduated from high school, I decided that I wanted to start my own business. I started a food distributing and manufacturing company. I had no money, just good companies that gave me credit. I had to convince suppliers to trust me, and that was my first hurdle. I was able to buy some pickles, mustard, and mayonnaise from a manufacturer in San Diego, and later, a 1949 Studebaker truck to make deliveries. That was the beginning of Kirby Foods.

My first sale in business to my first customer was $1.80 for two gallons of mustard. My fledgling company grew in sales extremely fast because of good products and good service. Later, a company by the name of Continental Food Service, a national company with general offices in Chicago, was buying up small companies across the nation. They approached me with an offer I could not refuse. I sold my company, Kirby Foods, to them in 1967, and I was able to retire. However, I decided to stay on as vice president in an advisory capacity for the Southern California division for the next ten years because I took a ten year payoff.

This book is separated into two parts. Part 1 is about my cowboy days. After retiring in 1967, I had a lot of free time. I was able to pursue my boyhood dream of becoming a cowboy, and with that came a lot of cattle herding, wrecks, and unforgettable experiences. Part 2 is about my post cowboy days. My wife Marilyn and I traveled the world and experienced its wonders. We also took part in different business endeavors. We had the time of our lives!

There are several reasons why I decided to write this book. The first being if you have a dream, go after it! Remember wearing a gun and holster around your waist when you were a little kid? And if you were lucky enough, your mom or dad would even buy you a cowboy hat and maybe some spurs to complete the outfit? Most kids, as they grew older, would change that childhood dream to one of becoming a fireman or a policeman—not me. My dream was to become a cowboy, and I made sure that I did just that.

I also wanted to encourage those who may be contemplating retirement or who may have just retired, that senior citizens are in demand for all kinds of interesting jobs. Don't go home, sit down in a rocking chair, and start rocking. Grab a grandkid, take off to see the country that's rich with historical landmarks; take them places they may have never seen. That old bucket is sitting there waiting for you to kick it.

Jack – 1933 – Mason City, Iowa. This is where it all started.

Acknowledgements

I would like to thank the following people who helped make this book a realty:

To Mr. Whitney Cineilus, for writing down what I dictated.

To Mr. Bob Candland, for editing my manuscript.

To Robin Martin and Taylor Martin, for typing many of the stories.

To Taryn Martin, for preparing the manuscript for the publisher.

To Paul Kirby, for writing the Book Synopsis.

PART 1

Slowly Becoming a Cowboy

My love for horses and cowboys probably started in the late 1930's. My dad bought me a pony in 1937. We lived on ten acres of ground where the Ryerson Concrete Company is located today. It was east of town on the old Highway 80. My horse's name was Tony. He was brown and white and about forty two inches tall. He had a very gentle disposition. I crawled all over him and he never kicked or bucked.

We had two cows that Stan, my brother, and I had to milk early in the morning. We had twenty head of hogs that we had to feed. We also had to feed the chickens and gather the eggs for Mom and then back to milking in the evening. Dad planted Milo Maze corn one year that we had to irrigate. When it was ready to harvest, we tied gunny sacks around our waist and then start at one end of the field cutting off heads of grain and putting them in the sack until they were full or too heavy to drag. We dumped the sacks in piles. Dad would pick up the piles of sacks and put them in his truck and we would start again, going down the rows, picking and cutting off the heads of corn. In between work, I would find time to play with "Tony Boy, Pony Boy" as I would call him.

During lettuce season, Dad would have three or four loads of lettuce delivered and dumped in the field for our calves and cows to eat. I would get on Tony bareback and run along-side the piles of lettuce. I would then act like I got shot and fall off my horse into the lettuce piles. Tony would run a little ways and stop, so I would go and get him and jump on his back, just to do it all over again. No chance of getting hurt in those piles of lettuce, but I sure would get dirty and smelly, especially after it spoiled in the sun for four or five days.

Dad sold products to restaurants and grocery stores. During the day, Mom made potato and macaroni salad that Dad would sell to the grocery stores. Another chore for Stan and me was to peel the boiled potatoes daily for Mom's salads. Stan and I also had another chore to do, and that was to load the truck for Dad for the next day on his route. He would hand us a list of products to put on his truck. He had a warehouse with products on the farm.

Now, back to my horse life. In the "30's" the theaters on Saturday afternoons had continuing serial stories along with full-length movie, newsreel, and cartoons. The continued serial movie was usually The Lone Ranger and Tonto or Hop-Along Cassidy. There were different movies with different cowboys such as Gene Autry, Tim Holt and Roy Rogers. These serials always ended with the star about to be killed in some way. So, we would have to come back the following Saturday afternoon and see how he would get out of his situation. All this for ten cents, and the popcorn was the same price. So, after the movies, I would go home and play "Cowboys and Indians" with my pearl-handled pistols in their holsters, one on each hip, and back to falling off into the lettuce piles. Soon I developed some interest in making a horse harness for Tony and would hook him up to something to just drag around. I went to the Shoe Cobbler's in town to get scraps of leather and other pieces and I made Tony a harness that would work. In the summers, my folks would put me on a Greyhound bus and sent me to my uncle's in Colorado from the age of eleven through age thirteen, which you wouldn't do today in this world we live in now.

I would stay with my uncles and cousins for about two or three months, and they had horses. I could ride them from one uncle's farm to the other uncle's farm. My Uncle Orin farmed with draft horses. He taught me how to harness a horse, the names of the straps, and how to drive them. I got to mow with Old Nick and Joe (his team) and then haul the hay into the barn area from the field. I would grab a hay hook for hay and then Old Nick would pull it up to my uncle through a pulley to the hay loft, so he would have hay to feed his cattle through the winter.

Uncle Orin and Aunt Eveline had two kids, my cousins Orin "Bud" and Jeanine. Uncle Wyatt and Aunt Frances also had two kids, Roger and Ruthie, all wonderful cousins whom I love dearly. The uncles were my mother's younger brothers, and their last name was Smith, as was my mother's maiden name. Another of my uncles I had in Montrose was Uncle Harlan and Aunt Arlyene. They had one daughter, Charlene. Uncle Harlan worked on heavy equipment and had no horses, but more on him later in the book.

In 1942, my folks sold our ten acre farm on Highway 80 to Ryerson Concrete Company, and when we moved to town, Dad bought a house at 734 Broadway. There was a vacant lot to the East. On the corner of the vacant lot lived two classmates of mine, Joanne and Donella Quinn. Of course I took Tony Boy with us to town. I built a small corral for him on the vacant lot next to us. My grade school was Wilson, located where the police station is today, at the corner 11th and Broadway. Across the street to the East, and North of the Courthouse, was a two-acre lot full of date palm trees and grass. I would hook Tony up and drive him to school, tether him to a palm tree and walk across the street to school. Then after school, I would throw the harness on him, hook him up to my cart and trot three blocks home. None of this could happen today, because of laws in our city or someone could steal him. This is what they mean by "the good ole days," the days when we could do things like this.

Wilson school burned during the summer of 1944 so, the eighth grade class had to go to school at Central Union High School for our eighth grade year. That lead to a lot of teasing over how it took our class five years to go through a four year high school.

The time came when I had to sell Tony Boy. When the man came to pick him up in his four-door car, I led Tony over to the car, opened the back door, and shut the doors after he was in. You are probably wondering how you could load a pony in the back seat of a car. Well, remember we're not talking about a four-door 2012 Mustang. The cars in the "30's" had large back doors with running boards that Tony stepped on and then on into the back seat floor board area and then I shut the doors. I collected my money and away he went. I never saw him again. I have often thought of what his back seat must have actually looked like once he got home with his cargo. Needless to say, my heart was broken to have given him up. I still think of him, and I thank God daily for giving me such a great boyhood and wonderful parents, but I knew my life would get much better. I had no idea what God had in store for me. Now, as I look back, I am able to see that He had a wonderful plan for my life.

First Meeting with My Best Friend

First, I want to tell you how I got interested in saddle horses and harness horses. Remember wearing a gun and holster set around your waist when you were a little boy? And if you were lucky enough, mom and dad would buy you a cowboy hat and maybe some spurs and some guy would come around leading a pony and take your picture on him with your hat, gun, and spurs. Then as you grew older you may have changed to wanting to be a fireman or a policeman. Well, I never changed. All my life I wanted to be a cowboy and work with horses. And my dream came true.

In 1967, I was on my way to Seeley when I saw a dark bay horse standing at the end of a pasture next to the highway. I immediately turned my car around. I walked over to the fence and called him, and he came to me. He let me pet him on the nose and stroke his head. I think it was love at first sight for the both of us, so I stopped by every day. If he was at the other end of the pasture, I would whistle and call him, and he would come on a trot. I knew that I had to own this horse.

I found out who owned him and bought him for $200. He was four years old, green broke, and fresh out of Texas. I asked Jack Nemo, the former owner, if there were any holes in him that I should look out for. Jack told me that there were none. He was as honest as you could ask for. I asked Jack what his name was, and he said *Tonka*. It was a Sioux Indian word meaning "strong one," and that he was.

I called my long time friend John Taylor who was a professional wrangler. He was in charge of as many as 8,000 head per year, and he moved the cattle in bunches of 500 at a time from field to field as he found pasture ahead of them. I asked John if I could go on a cattle drive with him someday. He said, "Yes. I'll call you." A few days later, he called me for my first cattle drive, and that was the start of being a big time cowboy.

My First Cattle Drive

The greatest experience of my life for the next 24 years was about to start, of course on my first cattle move. I had to start on the dusty drag at the end of the herd. The field was at the west end of Main and Austin Road. I arrived on time. John and the other boys were there and had already rounded up the herd. I stepped off my horse talking with John and he told me what to do on the drag; go back and forth keeping the stragglers going and not to stray too far behind.

We made the move with no trouble, and I talked to John after we entered the field. Sitting there on a horse, he told me I did a good job and was happy to have me aboard as a steady hand. He said he would call me for the next move.

When I started, we would go on cattle drives one or two days a week. But the closer Marilyn and I got to them, the more we would go out together. We started riding more and more, and John and I would only take the girls when they really wanted to go, which was most of the time. Sometimes, I was in the saddle six days a week, but very rarely. Saturday and Sunday, we were always off unless it was raining or storming. John and Vera started going to church with us every Sunday, and then Sunday after church, it was dinner at the Cameo. They became very close friends and neighbors.

My First Roped Steer

My second time out, Johnny called me and asked if I wanted to go check some cattle with him and Dickie Johnson down on Cole Rd, just northeast of Hartman Williams Feed lot, which was owned by Tom Remington. He was one of the nicest men that I have known. We took a lot of cattle over the years in and out of his feed yard. We arrived at the field and we unloaded our horses and rode out into the herd looking for a sick steer that we may have to rope and doctor. I was hoping we could find a sick animal so we could rope him. No luck. We started to leave, but before we got out of the field I told John and Dickie that I wanted to learn how to rope.

Dickie picked out one for me and told me what to do, "Don't give him more than one steer length in front of your horse. The closer the better. Keep him on the right side of your horse." I got one all lined out to rope, hit *Tonka* with my spurs and the race was on. I got him out where Dickie had told me and threw my loop and it sailed over his head, so I pulled up *Tonka* and coiled up my rope and picked out another steer for another try. He told me this time throw your rope down at the steer's head and not across his body. After a half dozen tries, I finally caught my first steer and then the next move was to dally my rope around my saddle horn. I was running along after the steer and Dickie was running along beside me, hollering instructions to me on how to dally and then pull up my horse and stop the steer. I did and then the steer and I were facing each other, both of us wondering what in the world was next.

Dick told me to turn my horse to the left and pull forward so he could rope his hind legs. He caught them the first try we stretched the steer out and he fell to the ground. Dick got off his horse while his horse held the rope tight. He walked up to the steer lying on the ground, put his knee on his neck and asked me for some slack. Then he slipped my rope off his head. He quickly got back on his horse, spooked the steer up, gave him some slack and his rope fell off of the steer's heels. After a high five and a big smile, I knew I was hooked.

Most Moves Were Fun and Easy

Not all our cattle moves were difficult ones, thank the Lord for that, because we would use a lot of greenhorns on the ones that we knew would be easy. Our pastor's wife, Gwen McGuire went with us a time or two and rode in the rear with the girls. Marilyn told me she was so funny. She would sing to the steers and talk to them and say "Come on boys, Jesus loves you." Harry Barnum didn't know a horse knew how to walk. He loved to run all the time chasing steers that would cut from the herd and stray off in a different direction. Sometimes, we would accuse him of deliberately cutting one out from the herd just so he could chase it down on a full run.

When Bob Kirby would come down from Oregon to visit us here in the Valley, he was always in the saddle when we had a move and was a good hand. Kenny Dukes would be out at the corrals when we were saddling up and loading our horses and wanted to go so bad, but we didn't always have enough horses to go around, so he bought himself a horse and saddle and would go with us every time he could go. Steve Scaroni was a good hand but couldn't go with us that often. He was full-time farming at that time. Of course, Cheryl and Kenna Taylor, John's two daughters, were called on in John's early years of wrangling when my brother would visit and we had a cattle move. Stan and his youngest son, Steve, would always go if we had enough horses. Steve sometimes rode our old friend *Dusty*, our Shetland pony. Stan Switzer and his two daughters helped us often when we would take a herd in or out of the Centinela Feed Yard down on Cole Rd. It was owned by Stan.

Pia Carlson and Britt Marie Swenson were foreign exchange students from Sweden, one in 1975 and the other in 1978. They loved to move cattle with us. Robin Kirby, our daughter, also would go when she could. Even Aunt Char Wardrup from Corona Del Mar, my sister-in-law, would even go with us. On one cattle move she got overheated and had to get off her horse and rest because it was a very warm day. Earl Bowler was from Gillette, Wyoming and he would spend his winters at Desert Trails. I met him at the Broken Spoke Golf Course. He was the only man around with a cowboy hat on so I walked up to him and introduced myself. I asked him if he was a cowboy or did he just find the hat? Come to find out, he was a cattle and sheep man all his life and had just turned the ranch over to family members. The Bowlers would come out for the winter to get away from the snow. He would bring his tack with him over the years.

Leland Raley was an old rodeo cowboy but was working for the Imperial Irrigation District and wasn't available, except on weekends. John would always make cattle moves weekdays and just go and check the wire around the fields. He would check the water and also make sure there were no steers walking outside the fence on Saturday and Sunday. Gerry Aulis was a retired minister from Boston. It was his boyhood dream to go on a cattle drive. He finally bought his own horse *Shasta* and tack and when we had a move he was there with his spurs and cowboy hat. When I would arrive and see him I would always say, "Hey fella, are you a real cowboy or did you just find that hat?" He would put his head down and shake it sideways and say, "Jack, I don't know about you!"

We were on a move from down about Calexico headed for the Kubler feed lot. That was down in New River bottom. Gerry and I were up on top of the river bank. Gerry was 100 yards or so ahead of me. I turned to check my steers behind me, and when I turned to look ahead Gerry was gone just that quick. I took off on a run to see what happened to him. When I got up to where I last saw him, there he was sitting on *Shasta* and she was lunging trying to get out of that hole they were in. The bank had given away under their weight and the cattle were getting closer to us. I knew I had to get him out quick. I threw Gerry my rope and pulled him out. Then we caved in some more of the bank on Shasta to where she could get a little footing and we were pulling on her bridle reins to help her finally get some footing and out she came. Gerry and I got back on our horses quickly just in time to check up on the herd and to continue on to the Kubler feed lot. "Good job, Gerry!" I rode up along side of him with a big high five.

How We Moved From Field to Field

Most of our cattle moves were within the five-mile range or less. Sometimes we would move from one side of the fence to the other side of the fence, which is sometimes much more difficult than one down the road. We always would come out of the corner of the field and down the road in the direction away from the field we are going in.

In other words, if we are going east to the next field we would go out the east corner of that field and the same if we were going west, then we would go out the west corner of the field, and the same for north and south. We would gather the cattle by sending two or three cowboys in to the field to gather the cattle towards the corner we wanted, and the cowboys waiting at the gate would start calling the herd by hollering loud like a steer would make if he was lost or looking for his mother, and here they come on a run and crowd the gate. It takes a couple of moves to get them to respond like this, but once they get it, it is easy to get them to come. We would leave the two or three cowboys in the field behind the herd. The open gates are about sixty feet wide and it is difficult to get 500 heads though that small hole. So the ones in the rear sometimes get impatient and want to turn and run back in the field. So that is why, we keep two or three hands inside the fence. To keep them calm and bunch up. The girls stay outside so they can fall in to the tail end of the herd. Then the two or three cowboys work their way through the herd to the front so they can drop off to close a hole or a cross road and keep them going, and then work their way to the front again after they all pass by the hole. Now when moving from a pasture to across the fence to an adjoining field, you have to have three or more hands on the inside of the new field to keep them going straight ahead so they can't double back on the inside fence line which will cause the steers which haven't left the field yet to follow the herd down the fence line and then the battle is on to keep them going through the open gate. Very tiring for a cowboy and his horse. Occasionally, one or two steers would break away from the herd leaving the field and we would have to chase him down. If they wouldn't come back to the herd, we would come back later with a horse trailer, rope him and drag him in to the trailer, load your horse in with him and take him into the new field, open the trailer gate and let him out, then calling him a few unkind words for causing us all the extra work; but actually we liked it because we would get to rope. Lots of fun.

Depending on the time of day, if it was close to lunch, we had four places we would go to: Camacho's, Mount Signal Café, the Cameo, or the De Anza Hotel coffee shop. There was always about five to eight cow hands. So they all liked seeing us come in with pockets full of money, cowboy hats, spurs, sweaty shirts, and dusty hats. Always... and a little manure on our boots. Gerry Aulis, being a retired minister, would say grace for us and would always ask for our safety on the dive. He always stood up and prayed loud enough that it would include the blessing on the whole restaurant and everyone in it. Of course, we all removed our hats. Of our favorite places, it was always Camacho's and it still is today. Marie, the owner had three daughters, Rosie, Diane and Cheryl and a waitress named Cynthia and they still wait on us, even today. I have a lot of fun teasing the girls of which one I like the best or which one is my favorite. Blanca was Marie's main cook, and I always would go to the kitchen and speak to Blanca in Spanish in the kitchen and she greets me back with a great smile. Writing about Camacho's has made me hungry. It's 5:00 p.m., so I'm on my way to dinner. Robin called and said her family and her son-in-law, Vic will join us with his wife Cheryl, their three kids Zachary, Alexandra and Victoria. So I'll save a table for ten as we do every Saturday night.

El Centro, California – Camacho's Place, located about 8 miles out of town, is a family-owned café that has been open for over 65 years. Photo courtesy of Paul Noden.

200 Head of Our Own

John and I bought 100 head each for ourselves. We had them delivered to Bob Lemon's Feed lot down on Cole Rd, near Calexico. They were small, maybe 250 or 300 pound babies, so we ran them through a pinch shoot. A pinch shoot is where you put a steer when you are going to doctor him. He runs his head through thinking he can go through, but just as soon as he gets in, we clamp the pinch shoot on his neck then the sides come in against him to where he literally can't move a muscle in any direction. Then all the procedures start on him. John would castrate, while I was branding him with a red-hot iron. 100 head for John and 100 head for me.

My brand was a bar "JK" on his left shoulder and John had several brands; I don't remember which one he used on his hundred. Then, I dehorned and vaccinated him all in about two minutes and turned him out. He was so glad to get out of there that I don't think he even felt the pain. It all happened so quick, of course. The smell of burnt hair was very strong in the air. The next little feller came down the lane and to the pinch shoot thinking he was going on through and oh, no!

Not until we were through with our work on them, and after all were treated with our branding and all, we fed them well and left them in the corral for about a week to let the soreness get out of them. Then we took them out to pasture and mixed them with another small herd. On the way to check the other herds, we swung by another feed lot and took about a bucket of testicles known as "mountain oysters" and gave them to the feed lot hands to take home for dinner. If you've never tasted a mountain oyster, you don't know what you're missing.

Then John and I would check the other herds and see that they had plenty of water. While we were there, we'd also make sure the fences were hot. To make sure the wire was up and working, we liked to drive around all four sides if we could. After that, it was home for a

Jack Kirby

good shower. John, Vera, Marilyn and I would go to the Cameo Buffet for dinner every evening if we weren't too tired. On the way home, we would swing by the feed lot and take a bucket of testicles, known as "mountain oysters," and give them to the feed lot hands to take home for dinner. If you've never tasted a mountain oyster, you don't know what you're missing.

Gifts for Mexico

We were moving a herd down the All American Canal bank before it was lined with concrete. It was just dirt banks in those days—U.S.A. on the north side, old Mexico on the south bank. On this particular day, two head walked down the bank to get a drink of water and wound up jumping into the canal. One turned back to us and climbed out, and the other swam across to the other side and climbed out on the Mexican side. He followed along on that side with the main herd on the USA side. We all figured we lost him to a taco factory in Mexico. I know this because we had it happen before, when one would swim south to Mexico.

On this day, we won out. He decided to come back to the USA and join the crowd. Maurice, John, and I were leading the herd. Marilyn and Vera were pushing on the drag as usual.

Maurice said, "John, I've got to urinate.", so I told him, "Maurice just lope your horse up there to those bushes and get behind them. The girls are way back there and would never know what's going on." Off goes Maurice. I saw him get off his horse up ahead and get behind the bush. Before he was through, John and I were getting close to him and so I hollered out, "Marilyn, bring that steer over here!" I know that was a mean joke to play on Maurice because there was no way Marilyn was close, but Maurice didn't know that. He was trying to take care of himself and in his hurry, wet all over himself.

He got up on his horse, saw the girls were still way back on the tail end and then he unloaded on me, "Jack, you ornery cuss! See what you caused!" pointing to his wet jeans. "I'll get even with you, don't worry!"

We finally get to the field, move them in perfectly just like they are supposed to go in, with no problems. Maurice and I got off our horses to shut the gate which is a single barbed wire.

Maurice said, "Jack, bring me the gate wire."

I replied, "Okay, is it hot?" (meaning if he had hooked it up to the electricity). He said, "No, not yet."

I reached down and grabbed the wire and 120 volts shot through my body. Now it didn't take me long to look at that wire. Maurice and John were bent over in laughter and Maurice said, "Now we are even, Jack." *Lesson learned.*

Practice Roping in Arenas

Dickie Johnson and Howard Smithers partnered up on a roping arena, and built it on Dickie's property. They put up lights so they could rope at night. John and I used to load up our horses and go over once a week to practice. They had a nice bunch of Corriente steers from old Mexico with nice horns, so we could team rope. John and I would take turns, roping the head, the other roping the heels. It wasn't just practice but a lot of fun with other cowboys. We would back our horses into the chutes with the steer in the center and sit there a minute while *Tonka* would gather his feet under him. I could feel his heart beating through my saddle as he was anticipating an explosion out of the chute. John and I would look at each other with our ropes coiled and ready to circle our heads and make the catch. When we were all ready, we would nod our head and the man on the gate would release the steer and the race was on.

The header would always make the call after the header was certain the steer was pointed straight in the chute and not with his head down or doubled back. The header would catch the horns and turn his horse off to the left and then the heeler would slip right in close to the steer's left hip. As the header would pull the steer at a lope, it would cause the steer to hop as he pulled back against the rope. As he was hopping, the heeler would then have a chance to throw his big loop under the belly between the front legs and the back legs. That's where the heeler would jerk his slack, dally his rope and stop his horse and pull back. The header would stop his horse and turn him to the left and face the heeler. If you had a timer in the arena when the ropes were tight on both ends and the ropers were facing each other, he would drop the flag, stopping the clock for your time.

John and I would go to different arenas for practice and fun: the 3D Cattle Yard, Wayne Medland, Dickie's Arena, my arena at home, and the Brawley Cattle Call for competitive roping up against the cowboys that worked cattle all over the northern and southern parts of the Imperial Valley. I'm proud to say the best I ever did competitively was third place. I was heading and Johnny Johnson was heeling. He was Dickie Johnson's youngest son. I didn't start roping until I was in my forties, when I built our home out on McCabe Road and I had my own arena. My father-in-law, Burl Wardrup and John Taylor would come over and we would rope together. Wes, the number two son would come out occasionally and rope with me. Speaking of Wes, he and his best friend Craig "Columbo" Reichert came out to Dickie's arena one night and the both of them, big high school football stars, wanted to bulldog steers. So, we had them stand alongside the gate where the steers come out. They would grab him by the horns and dig their heels in the dirt and bring a 700 pound steer to a stop and twist his head to the right till the steer would fall to the ground. Man, did we have some laughs watching them do that. Sometimes the steers would get the best of the contest. At home in our arena, Wes would race me for fifty yards. He's on foot and I'm on *Tonka*, 25 yards up to the line, stop, turn, and 25 yards back to the finish. He would usually beat me and *Tonka*. It was always close because he could stop and turn around on his way back to the finish much quicker than me and old *Tonka*.

Paulie our oldest son, thoroughly loved his time with *Dusty* and our buggy, but after a few years went by, both boys got interested in motorbikes. When that happened, Robin took over *Dusty*. I had just bought *Tonka* and we went out camping overnight. Robin and I rode *Tonka* and the boys rode their motorbikes up and down the hills all day. There was a great camp fire that evening, cooking hot dogs and marshmallows. The next morning, a little more fun riding, then we loaded up for home on Brighton Ave.

I took *Tonka* home to where I had bought him. I was still boarding him there until I could find a place to move him. After we got hooked up with John Taylor, I moved Tonka to another place. The boys continued on more and more with their dirt bikes and became big league with it. Paul after many serious crashes, a mashed in face, and a broken neck with a steel plate in his number four and five vertebrae, he slowed down with his racing but was president of his desert riding club. He set up many desert races and still does it at this time in his life. Our son Wes, crashed the next year after Paulie and broke his neck. There's a steel plate in his neck in his number five and six vertebrae. They had to redo Wes's plate a few years later and fused vertebrae number five, seven, and eight with another plate. He quit altogether after the first surgery, but after a few years it deteriorated and he had to do it all over again. The same surgeon did both boys and had enough money from the surgeries to retire.

Paulie's son, Bobby got into dirt bike desert racing and became a champion, earning the number one plate, "Desert Racer of the Year, District 38, of Southern California." He also rode for the Honda Team in the Baja 1000-mile race and finished on his leg fourth overall, bikes and cars. The other team riders had some troubles and finished 82nd overall out of 450 entries. That is cars and bikes. Bobby has crashed several times, broken collar bones, once on the left and once on the right. One bad crash ended in a life flight to the San Diego Trauma Center. Now, he wants to fly helicopters.

Paulie and Bobbie still ride in the desert and in fact they are heading out there this weekend. Wesley went on to be a golf club professional. Bobbie went on and became a CIF, a semi-finalist, for his high school in golf and played against Anthony Kim who is on the PGA Tour today. Bobbie is also an excellent calf roper on my electric calf roping machine.

I enjoyed calf-roping the best, it was more physical and you depended on your horse so much to keep the rope tight so the calf could not get away from you. After you caught the calf, stop your horse, hard jump off while he was sliding to a stop. After that, run down the rope to the calf with your left hand on the rope and put your right hand on the flank of the calf. Pick him up off his feet and slam him to the ground. Take your tie down rope which is called a Piggin' String, from your mouth, and put the left loop over his right front leg. Grab his back two legs and pull them up over the front leg. Two wraps with the tie down and pull the end back through the last wrap, which is called a Hooey, and then throw your hands in the air for your time. I did this at my own arena and down the road to Hank Gorham's arena as well as at our Kiwanis Gymkhana's Fund Raiser held every year at the Brawley Cattlecall Arena. Old *Tonka* was so good at this procedure. I had him trained to keep the rope real tight while I was tying the calf. When I would rope alone, I would stand up after the tie, snap my fingers and *Tonka* would step towards the calf and release the pressure on the rope, so I could take the rope off and do it all over again.

One Friday evening after practice roping at Johnson and Smithers Arena, John and I loaded our horses and drove home after having a lot of fun with our fellow cowboy friends. We found out the next morning that after Dick and Howard got all their cattle fed and watered and turned out. They turned out the arena lights. Howard loaded his roping horse in his trailer, shut the tailgate and started home. About two miles into his way home, he stopped at the stop sign at Aten and Dogwood Roads, and then proceeded in his way, not knowing that when he shut the tailgate on his trailer, it did not latch. When he had stopped at the sign, the gate opened and his horse backed out while he was stopped. Howard went on home only to find his horse missing. He immediately turned around and started back the way he came. He arrived at Aten and Dogwood only to find a car had hit and killed his horse. Not expecting to see that and hoping for the best it was an awful sight to come upon.

After the boys closed the arena, I had sold the farm and my horses. I purchased an electric, automatic roping horse from a manufacturer in New Mexico. He had made a fiberglass horse mounted on a steel frame and a little fiber glass calf on wheels mounted on a 16 foot track under the horse. I put a saddle on him. When you wanted to rope your calf, you would kick the horse on the right side which would engage the motor on the calf and down the track it would go. Then you would rope him before he reached the end of the track. Three seconds after you caught or missed the calf, it would return to its position under the horse. I would lean, take the rope off, and go again. *Excellent practice.* It was very cheap to operate; no hay and no manure to shovel. My last roping horse I had was named *Slick,* so I named this machine *Oil Slick* because all I had to do was oil him once in a while.

So You Wanna Be a Cowboy?

Yeah! That's me practicing my calf roping with Tonka holding my rope tight.

Johnny Johnson moving in to pick up the heels in the Calf Call competition. We took third place—not too bad for an old guy and a kid.

Jack Kirby

This is me roping a mechanical calf on my mechanical horse, Oil Slick.

Michael's Invention for Moving Cattle

Mike Taylor helped us whenever we needed, but Mike was one that was always thinking of ways to do things, or build something that could or would make his work or life easier. So, he built this contraption to attach to a pickup. He made it out of PVC plastic pipe. It would fold forward up along side of the pickup so you could drive on a road. When using it to hold back a herd of steers while moving on a road, it would unfold at a 90 degree angle on both sides of the truck, about 30 feet on each side. If you have ever seen horse harness racing it looked like what they use to start the race when extended.

We had a two-mile straight move down Willoughby Road. At the end of the road we were to turn to the right, go across a bridge over the Willoughby Canal, then north on Clark Rd to the first canal crossing on the left. We then go down that dirt path to the next field and in the pasture. This contraption, Mike said the pickup would start in front of the herd with the arms extended out from the pickup. Then he wanted John on one side and me on the other. We were to keep the herd behind the extended arms. Now, the idea kind of sounded maybe, but it certainly didn't work like Mike had planned it. I still can't believe to this day that John let us try it out on our cattle. All hands were grinning including me the whole time Mike was explaining how this was going to work. He said he was going to patent the device and change cattle moving forever.

Well, we were bringing our usual, about 500 head or so out of El Toro and going south on Ware Road. We went across the Willoughby Canal bridge, and then a 90 degree turn to the right, now going west where old Jim McDaniels was waiting in a pickup with Michael's invention on it, all spread out across the road anticipating the cattle. Now, Jim McDaniels was all crippled up in his hands and talk tongue-tied. He also hadn't driven a vehicle in years. Jim lived in the hotel across the street in the rear of the Cameo and ate all his meals there.

That's where I met him and he was always after me to go on a cattle drive. He couldn't ride a horse, but he could follow the move in a pickup, which would save us from riding back to get the trailers. He didn't have a driver's license, but there sat Jim ready to go when we holler, "Go! Go!" We did, and Jim started moving.

We were about 200 yards into the move when Jim slowed down too much for some reason. The cattle up close to the wings ducked their heads down and started to run underneath the thing on both sides of the truck. When they did that thing started flopping and breaking up, making a lot of noise with pieces flying everywhere. So, we finally got Jim to stop. Now, the herd was racing away in a stampede. It was two miles to Clark Road and our next turn to the north on it. Johnny and I took off on a dead run as hard as we could go to get ahead of the cattle before the turn. We got there just ahead of them and got the leaders bumped to the right, turning them over the bridge and now going north on Clark Road. Johnny hollered at me to catch the leaders again and try to turn them to the left at the next canal crossing. I heard him say that his horse was shot and there was no way he could catch them. I was riding *Freckles* that day and he still had a little left in his tank, so off I go with the cattle, crossing the bridge. I buried my spurs in his ribs and he gave me all he had. We passed the leaders. They saw me standing there at the dirt trail crossing the canal and before they got to me, they bailed off in that little canal and out on the other side across the field, west in the direction that we wanted to go. They were all spread out across that field.

By now, Maurice, Mike and Gerry had arrived. We all fanned out in the field and got them all headed up again. I loped on down to the pasture where we were going. The gate was open and I started calling them while the boys kept pushing them to me. The stampede was over finally, and better than I was expecting it to. Jim was there with the pickup and what was left of Mike's invention. He took me back to get a trailer at El Toro, and then back to pick up the men and horses. The men were walking the cattle to the water drinkers. When they finished we all loaded up the horses and stood there laughing at Mike's invention and how bad the move could have been. All our horses were shot and ready to go home after that two-mile run. John and I saddled some fresh horses and went back to check the other herds while the rest of the men went home. Michael recovered from all the teasing and started immediately to work on his next idea.

Lost Antique

We were receiving a herd on alfalfa pasture just northeast of Calexico. They were unloading them off of a truck rather than driving them. It would have been too far to drive them. They were a good gentle herd, so no problems unloading them. They just went right off the truck into the field and started eating which always makes an easy move, so *we* can get to lunch early.

John saw one steer come down the chute that looked sick. He said, "Kirb, rope that steer. He looks sick to me, so I'll give him a shot." So, I separated him from the herd and got him to about the middle of the field. I hit *Tonka* with my spurs and in about three jumps, I had him caught. Maurice came and picked up the heels and we stretched him out. John walked over on his horse, jumped off of *Cannon*, and got his needle and bottle of medicine that he always carries on the back of his saddle. He filled his syringe, dropped his reins to the ground, and old *Cannon* just stood there. John walked over and gave the bovine a shot in the rear. Then he did the normal procedure with his knee on the critter's neck and I gave him some slack. He then removed my loop from his head. Then Maurice gave him some slack on his end. The steer got up, stepped out of the loop and just walked off. I knew he was sick, 'cause he didn't try to run when he got up. We went back to load our horses and I noticed my belt flapping with no buckle.

My buckle was an antique worth a lot of money, given to me as a Christmas gift from Aunt Char, my sister-in-law. It was very valuable and I didn't ever want to lose that thing. So, I and a couple of hands went out to the center of the field to where I remember about where I was when I roped that steer. We all looked around the best we could but the alfalfa was too thick and tall. There was no way we could see the ground to find the buckle. John said that after they eat the field down in a couple of weeks we could then walk the field in that area and maybe we can find it.

Three weeks later, we went back to move the herd. John, Gerry, and I went out there. We got about five feet apart and began to walk our horses slowly in the area where I lost it. Lo, and behold we walked up on it and there it was laying there face up, a small miracle. It is still hard to believe that we found it that easy. What caused me to lose it, was when I roped the steer I leaned forward as I always do, standing up in the stirrups. When I did, the saddle horn apparently bumped the buckle and caused the buttons holding it to my belt to come unbuttoned, and letting it fall to the ground. *All's well that ends well.* We rounded 'em up, and out the gate and down the road to the next field.

It was another day of fun and lunch at the Cameo. John and I were the only ones that went there that day. Jimmy, my manager had hired a new waitress that had no idea who I was. John and I took our plates into the dining room to eat because they were not using it and we were a little dusty with some manure on our boots and our spurs. I didn't want to sit out front with the lunch crowd so we went into that room away from everyone. We were eating away when in comes the new girl and says, "You fellas can't eat in this room, it's closed." I told her why we were eating in there. She replied, "I'm sorry sir, you will have to go out front." "Okay.", I replied. We picked up our plates and moved out front. Jimmy told her later on who I was, and she stayed away from me whenever I was in the buffet. She acted kind of like a coyote. Bless her heart; she was just doing her job.

Stampede from Heber to El Centro

John, Marilyn, Vera and I took our horses down to Heber to the El Toro Feed Yard. I talked with Jiggs Johnson, the owner of El Toro, while his men were getting our herd ready to go out to pasture with us and getting a count. Now John and I were to be up front and the girls were all set to bring up the rear. It was supposed to be an easy move with gentle cattle that had been moved several times and knew what we were going to do with them. It seemed we were moving nice and slow out the gate with no crossroads that had to be blocked.

Now, the girls had been complaining in the truck all the way from home and after we arrived they were still whining about why they couldn't go up front in the lead and the guys would take the tail end for a change. So John, bless his heart, gave in and let the girls take the lead. All was going well, John had his fence crew string up barb-wire on the right to keep them out of that field and a canal was on the left. We came to a 90 degree turn to the north, then alongside of a long row of eucalyptus trees with a lot of dead branches, twigs, and leaves on the ground. The cattle began jumping the branches and breaking the twigs, and rattling the branches with leaves on them, and it spooked the herd. They began to run, passing the girls on both sides of them. They were trying to get them stopped but couldn't. John and I saw what was happening up front with the girls, so John and I took off to try to get in front of them and shut 'em down before we get to Heber Rd, which is a busy road. Thank the Lord the lead steers got to the road in between cars. The cars coming from both directions saw the cattle running across the road, and they all stopped while the herd was running. They were moving fast with no one up front, going straight ahead and up on the canal bank on the other side of the road. John and I were trying to go through them as fast as we could. By now, the girls were back on the drag. We had a canal on the left and a fenced-in field on the other side, so Johnny and I couldn't go out around them to get to the lead.

I put *Tonka* right in behind John. We were making progress slowly to the front. The next crossroad was three miles up ahead. They were all running unchecked. At the next crossroad, it was a jog to the right, and right back to the left. There was no way they could have made that move without a man there on a horse to push them one way, then in about fifty yards push them back left again. They had been running now for over three miles as fast as they could but they were tiring and slowing down some, which allowed us to gain on them. We finally caught up with the front leaders just in time, but we still had to stop them so we could bunch them up. They were strung out a mile long. The girls were bringing up the drag on a slow lope.

After we successfully made the second jog to the left, there was a wet field of alfalfa on our right. So we turned them which brought them to an immediate stop, while the rest of them finally caught up. The field we were going to was a quarter of a mile down the road. The girls finally showed up with streams of tears flowing down their dusty cheeks and both of them were saying, "We're sorry. We just couldn't hold them." Of course, we started teasing them that the whole stampede started because of them. We told them they were talking about the color of their nails, and their hairdo's, and where they would go to dinner that night. Needless to say, that didn't set too well with them, but they never asked again to take the lead.

We got them rounded up and out of the field and on down to the next pasture, which was a wheat field that later became the Desert Trails Resort. We shut the gate, loaded our horses, and headed home without a word being said from the girls in the back seat. Little did I know that the next year we would build the Broken Spoke Golf Course in the center of the Desert Trails Resort. After the golf course was created, I stood back and looked at what I had accomplished with one of his greatest creations—the horse. Tom and Jerry, my Clydesdales, were used to level out the ground and float the greens. That was real horse power! There were little hills, four ponds, and a creek—I was ecstatic at how it turned out. I thought for a while as I gazed upon what I had built. I said to myself, "If I am this ecstatic over this little job, I wonder how God must have felt when He looked at what He had built. Mountains, rivers, and oceans.

Aerial view of the future Desert Trails R.V. Park and Broken Spoke Country Club.

1985 – Finishing up some areas on the golf course with Tom and Jerry.

1985 – Finishing up some areas on the golf course with Tom and Jerry using real horse power.

Aerial view of the completed Desert Trails R.V. Park and Broken Spoke Country Club.

Twelve Mile Move

We all gathered at John's Corral at 8:00am. It was John, Mike, Maurice and Vera, and Marilyn and I. We put three horses in John's trailer and three in mine, and down the road we went to the field, southeast of the Mount Signal Cafe. Six cow hands and their horses were heading for a ride not to be expected, and little did we realize it would be so tiring and hard, on man and beast.

By the time we unloaded and opened the gate. We got our two hands in the field to round up the herd and get them started towards the gate where John and Maurice were waiting for them. Marilyn and Vera were waiting for them to get to the gate also, but in their position for the tail drag. Mike and I loped our horses to the back of the field to get them started towards the gate. John saw that we had a good gathering and let them go out. The girls stayed back so they could fall in behind on the drag.

After they were out, Mike and I moved through the herd carefully, so as not to start a stampede. We got to the front with John and Maurice and started on our way to Highway 98, closing off holes on both sides of the herd along the way. Thank the Lord, they were a very docile herd and had been moved several times before and learned how to follow the lead horses.

We finally got to Highway 98, made the left turn to the west, and got around the corner with no problems, on our way to Drew Rd. When cars would come along and needed to pass, three of us would crowd the herd over to one side so traffic could pass slowly through the herd. We asked the drivers of oncoming cars to just sit and don't honk or make any noise, and the steers would pass on both sides of them without incident. There was not much traffic at all on Highway 98. The cattle moved along very well. There were still no problems and finally we reached Drew Rd. We turned the herd right to the north, and up on a canal bank. We were still moving good, just a little slower now. We are about three hours into the move from roundup time and out the gate.

The more the time went by and the miles dragged along, the cattle kept getting slower and slower and began to stray away from the rest of the herd, so Mike and I would lope out and bring them back to the herd. When they get real tired, it seems as if they go brain dead and just wander off in a different direction. The cowboys riding the sides of the herd really had to work hard now to keep them all together. The lead hands became bored because the cattle quit pushing them hard forward and the hands on the drag were getting busier back and forth pushing stragglers that were so tired. They couldn't, or didn't want to keep up. One steer on my side broke from the herd and wandered off to the left. I took off to gather him up and bring him back where he belonged. The faster my horse and I went, of course the steer did too, but I finally got around him, and turned him back at a lope. We came to a small ditch that had grown over with grass. The steer saw it and jumped. Old *Tonka* and I were bumping him on his rear end with *Tonka's* chest. *Tonka* nor I never saw the ditch. *Tonka's* front legs went in all the way up to his chest and then end over end we went. I landed on my back with my feet in the air and here came *Tonka's* hind end right at me. Thank the Lord his rear end hit my feet that were up in the air and knocked me right out of his way or I would have been as flat as a pancake. We both gathered ourselves to our feet and shook a little bit. I was so mad at that steer, I almost lost my religion.

I got back on *Tonka*. Caught up with the steer and got him back in the herd. Then I began to smile when I asked the crew if they saw that wreck. I got a big laugh from the boys and especially the girls that were watching me crash. It wasn't long until Mike had one on his side of the herd stray off for no reason at all, so Mike took off after him.

Now Mike wanted to have some action, so he decided to rope the steer instead of bringing him back. Off they go on a run. He threw his rope and caught the steer, but couldn't make his dally. He was holding on to the rope with his hands and the steer launched him out of his saddle. His horse and the steer ran off with the rope around the steer's neck, dragging out behind him. I checked on Mike to see if he was okay and then took off to rope the steer. I held him until Mike caught his horse and came over to where I was while the steer was standing. I rode around behind him with the rope now around his neck and behind his rear legs. Then I stuck my spurs deep in *Tonka's* ribs and jerked the legs out from under the steer. While he was down, Mike jumped off his horse and held the steer down with his knee on the steer's neck, took both of our ropes off. We coiled up our ropes and got back up on his horse. We drove the maverick back out to the herd where he belonged and continued on down the road, towards our destination, which was the Hugh Lyon's Ranch on Graham Rd; with incidents on our move we finally arrived at our destination. After getting them in the new field, a few started eating, but many of them laid down to rest. All hands knew how they felt because we all felt the same way, especially the girls on the drag.

We all went in Hugh's house and refreshed ourselves with a glass or two of cold water. We walked outside to where we had tied our horses and they were waiting to go home for a drink of water too, along with hay and a generous serving of grain. To our surprise and laughter, when we walked out, there on the ground lay Marilyn's horse, *Bucko*, all stretched out, saddle and all, pooped out as all of us were. Two of us got a ride back to the field that we had left several hours ago.

We got our trucks and trailers and back to Lyon's Ranch where we picked up the crew and horses and headed home. It was dark when we got home. I unloaded the horses that belong to John, and Marilyn and I went home. I let her out at the house. I went on down the lane to the barn and parked the rig, unloaded the horses, took off their tack and put them in their pens. I watched them roll and roll while I was feeding them. It had to feel good to get that saddle off. I walked up the lane to the house took a great shower and went to bed. I don't think I moved till morning. That was the longest drive we ever made.

Move from Hartman Williams Feed Lot

We were taking a herd from Hartman Williams in Calexico out to pasture. We were short-handed that day so, Manuel, one of the cowboys that worked for Hartman Williams was helping us. Manuel rode a small sorrel-colored horse with super cattle knowledge, well broke and lots of action. John and I were always trying to buy him from Manuel because he was such a good horse and always gave you 100 percent.

Manuel was riding up front with John, Maurice, and I. We kept asking him to sell us his horse, so he went into showing us how much action he had on his front feet. He started bouncing him back and forth, then left and right. All of the sudden, the horse staggered to the right into the bar ditch and backed up on the road with us in the lead. He dropped over on his left side, right on Manuel's leg, dead from a heart attack. Manuel was hollering for help, but we couldn't help him because we were one man short up front. Now, Johnny hollered back at him and said, "Hey, Manuel! I don't want to buy him now!"

I got up front and got busy trying to help hold the herd together. They were getting spooked at Manuel lying there on the ground with his horse on his leg, asking for help. When the herd had passed him, one of the hands on the tail drag stopped and pulled Manuel out from under his horse. We were close to Hartman Williams, so one of the cowboys put him on the back of his horse and gave him a ride back to the feed lot where he got a front end loader tractor. He came back loaded Manuel's dead horse in the front and took him back to the feed lot where he took off his tack and dumped his horse on the dead pile, which every feed lot has. A dead pile is where they place their dead animals and then the rendering company comes by and picks them up every other day or so and hauls them off for the hides, and dog food for the rendering plants.

We all felt sorry for Manuel. He loved that horse. When you're involved with animals, anything can happen at any time. We were glad that he wasn't chasing a steer on a dead run. That would have been disastrous. His leg was okay, not broken, but scraped up a little.

Another Move Down Highway 98

We were moving down Highway 98 with a full crew and 500 head all moving well, keeping them up against the canal so traffic could pass by. I remember one car blocked by the cattle, rolled down his window slapping his hand on the side of his car. We asked him to stop making noise because the cattle were jumping into the canal and some were running in the wrong direction.

John rode up alongside of him and said with a loud, angry voice, "I said stop and be quiet!" Again, he mouthed off at John. He shouldn't have done that. Johnny threw his coiled up rope at him through the window of his car and hit him in the face. That had to hurt, but I mean to tell you that really made the brakes come on at once. Some of the hands had gathered the herd and held them until we could get those out of the canal. Maurice roped one and pulled him out of the ditch, and the steer began to run sideways and ran into the side of the same car that the driver who had mouthed off to John was in. So now, that guy finally got to go with two memories from passing through a cattle herd: a fat lip from a rope and a dent in the side of his car from one of the steers that he had spooked into the ditch. I threw my rope around one steer and began to pull him out. I was riding my horse, *Freckles* that day. The steer was really too heavy for one horse, but *Freckles* was giving it his best. His belly was almost touching the ground. He was pulling so hard that my breast strap broke. (The breast strap holds the saddle from sliding back.) Well, my saddle slipped off over his rump and down his hind legs as he stepped from everything, leaving me still in my saddle and stirrups, sitting on the ground with no horse under me and looking foolish. Old *Freckles* was off and running to the nearest farmhouse. So, I continued to help the rest of the boys that had a rope on the steer to take it off for them. We had one hand following the herd with a pickup and trailer. After we got them all out of the canal, I threw my tack in the pickup and went for Freckles. I got myself back on him and took off on a run to catch up with the move. Lunch that day was at the De Anza Hotel coffee shop. Good food!

Tonka Jr. is to the left. Britt, our foreign exchange student from Sweden, is saddled up next to him on Tonka.

Britt is on Tonka Jr. She's helping Marilyn and Vera on the drag.

Haythorn Ranch: Ogallala, Nebraska

One summer at Cheyenne, we had finished our tour of duty there driving their old wild horses. A young man that ate lunch with us every day was also a contestant in the steer busting event. He would bring over from his ranch in Ogallala, four or five teams every year for the parades off his 80,000-acre ranch. He did all his farming with Belgian teams. I got acquainted with Craig Haythorn over the years and it so happened this year, he invited Stan, Viv, my brother-in-law, Carl Howland, my sister-in-law, Betty Howland, Marilyn and I to come over to Ogallala and stay a night or two at the ranch. Ogallala is another historical town that was on the Oregon Trail where travelers would stop for supplies, load up their wagons and then go on their way west. He parked us down by the barn, hooked us up with power and water, and asked us down to his house for dinner that night and a tour of his home which was a converted barn. It was huge and very well remodeled.

Craig was the third generation to own the ranch. We left the Haythorn's after dinner and went back to the RV. When we got back, we noticed the lights on in the arena that he had there by the barn, so we went over to see what was going on. The cowboys that worked on his ranch were team roping after their dinner. The cowboys I was talking to told me, some of the hands go down to the arena and rope for recreation about three nights a week. He told me about the live-in bunk house there on the ranch. I remembered passing it on the way down to the barn. I knew that they would have a cook at the bunk house, so I got up at five, and drove down there. Stan and Carl didn't go. I walked in the front door and the first thing I saw as I walked in was a huge round table with twelve chairs and a Lazy Susan in the middle, loaded with spices, jelly, jams and honey, and of course, some Tabasco sauce. A woman said to me, "What do you want for breakfast, fella?" I guess she thought I was a new hand, so I ordered up real good. I finished up before all the hands showed up and went back to the barn. One hand was there and told me where they would be working today.

When the time came, I went over there to watch them. They had mowed the rolling hills covered with prairie grass and were raking it this morning. They would bring it to a stacker who would lift it up on top of the stack with his team and a come along. *No tractors!* It was all being done with teams of horses, now that's my kind of life. I met a guy and we were talking about the Old West. He told me the shovel won the West, and I told him, "Sorry the horse won the West. If it wasn't for horses that shovel wouldn't have gotten out here." *Case closed!*

Rainstorm on Highway 111

It was raining hard and the wind was blowing. We all had our rain slickers on. We had moved all the other herds into their dry lots or feed yards. Our last move of the day was this herd on the corner of Ross and Highway 111, three miles east of El Centro and seven miles north of Calexico. The closet feed yard was the Allied Feed yard about five miles from where we were. John decided that we would take them out the northwest corner of the field. The field was on the east side of the freeway, which meant that we would have to get them out of the field as quickly as possible, so that when we turn south, down the freeway, the ones still in the field wouldn't double back on us.

The plan was to gather them all up in the corner and take down a lot of fence, making the gate out huge on Ross. We could then get the steers all out of the field before we turned south on 111. The next part of the plan was when we got to the freeway, I-8, that runs east and west, we would take them up the west bound off ramp across I-8 and down the on ramp and back on the 111 highway. Just thinking that the cattle could see sky all the way would be easier than to send them under the underpass, with traffic making noise above them. We had that kind of experience before.

We all agreed the plan was a good one so we started out rounding up the herd and bringing them to the corner. We got them all bunched up and let down the wire fence and the boys brought them all out at once heading west towards Highway 111, on the northbound lanes. The cattle were hungry, wet, and cold and wanted to run, but we had our best cowboys that morning, thank the Lord, and headed towards the I-8 freeway. The plan was going good as planned when up the off ramp, something spooked them and the herd split. Half of them were up the ramp and the other half towards the underpass bridges that left me alone with those going under the underpass. I knew I couldn't turn them back alone, so I went to hollering loud to get them going under there fast. Now, I had cattle on both the north and southbound lanes, so I ran *Freckles* up the steep bank on I-8, and got the traffic stopped for John's herd that was crossing over the top. I ran down the steep bank on the other side of I-8 and then down 111 to get in front of all of them that were coming underneath and the ones coming over the top. I got them slowed down so John's bunch could merge with the underpass bunch. I had gotten them all on the northbound lanes now.

One guy in a pickup going north stopped dead still instead of moving slow and passing the herd. It was cold and rainy and I saw his windshield was fogged over inside the cab of his truck, so he probably figured it would be better to stop than to go. I could see four more cars coming towards him. In my opinion, all were driving too fast for that kind of weather and too close to each other. The first one ran into the back of the guy that had stopped. *Freckles* heard the crash and jumped sideways. It felt like twenty feet at least. Then three more crashes. *Boom! Boom! Boom!* Five of them piled up and *Freckles* would jump every time they hit. We couldn't help anybody or we would have a stampede on the freeway instead of a controlled move in lousy weather.

It wasn't long before a Highway Patrol car pulled up alongside of me and asked if these were my cattle, in a mean tone of voice. I answered him, "No!"

"Well who's in charge then?"

"The guy up there on that buckskin horse." So, he drove up to John got out of his car all his lights flashing and said, "You want to get off your horse, so I can fill out my report?" Now here we are with 500 head of steers on a fast trot in a storm and he wanted John to stop, get off his horse and fill out a report. You can guess what he wanted to tell that officer!! What he did tell him was, "If you want to talk to me we are headed for the Allied Feed yard about five miles south on this highway." The officer mumbled a few more remarks, got in his car and took off back to the accident. We finally got to the Allied Feed lot and got them in their corral to stay until after the storm and then take them out to another pasture. The next thing that happened was John got a notice that the guy that stopped in his truck sued John's insurance company for $500,000.00. John's insurance company handled it. The other four cars didn't sue John, but probably sued each other. It was amazing how quick the neck brace came off after he collected the $500,000.00.

New Calves on Sudan Grass

Roy Smith and I met at John's Corrals about 7:00am one morning. Just the three of us were working that day. We left John's ranch to turn out 500 head of first time calves. They were about 400 pounders in weight that had never been out on pasture. They had been in feed lots since babies. Now Roy was riding my horse *Tonka Jr.*, and I was on *Tonka* and John was on his old faithful, big and powerful, dun in color, named *Cannon*. Little did we know or expect what was about to happen to three cowboys. It wasn't long and we had decided we needed a dozen or more cow hands. The evening before, we setup portable corrals in the corner of the field. A procedure we always use when we have first time calves. We let them stay all night in the pen, get good and hungry, and then normally three or four hands would ride out in the fields to slow them down if they wanted to run.
They usually would run out a little ways and stop, and then start to eat. Then we would walk them around all four sides of the pasture, so they could touch the one strand of electric wire and learn quickly to stay back away from that thing, because that wire hurt. We would walk them around the pasture until we came to the drinker. Now the calves had learned where the water is in the field, and don't touch that wire! We would always put one cowboy outside the fence just in case one calf decided to jump the wrong way after he touch the electric wire, and with new calves that would happen occasionally. Then the hand outside would have to rope him and bring him back and bring him through the gate.

    Well here goes one of the most exciting days of my cowboy career. We were all three in place. Roy was outside the fence, I was out in the pasture, and John was off his horse opening the gate to the portable corral. He then mounted old *Cannon* quickly and moved out on the field close to me where we could slow them down if they wanted to run. Now, the pasture was sedan grass, five and six feet tall. Normally, we would set new calves on alfalfa which isn't so tall and they could see each other and settle right down.

Well these calves started out of the corral slow and touching the tall sedan grass. As they moved out into the field they lost vision of each other, but they could hear each other making noise which ultimately scared them, hearing the noise but they couldn't see anything or a horizon. The grass was so tall; they took off in all directions. John and I did not know which way to go because they were all scattered through the field. Roy ran down to the far end of the pasture ahead of the stampede. Thank goodness, we had mowed about fifty feet of the grass all around the field. When they came out of the tall grass they could see that hot wire fence and hopefully stop. Well John and I, along with Roy outside the fence, pretty well got them stopped. However several head ran through the fence, forty-one to be exact, at the far end of the field and down a dirt road. All forty-one head were going. John pulled one fence stake out that was holding the wire off of the ground, and laid it down so we could get out of the field with our horses. He put the fence back up and we took off after the runaways. It was a very hot morning and with so much running our horses were wet with sweat and white with lather on their necks and chest. *Tonka* had a kidney problem. When he gets too hot like that and all lathered up his kidneys lock up and he can't even walk, let alone run. There was a tree in the middle of the field next to the pasture, where our herd was. I coaxed *Tonka* to the shade of that tree very slowly, little tiny steps, and left him there just standing. I didn't even tie him up. I had no needle or lasix with me to help relieve his pain. A shot of that stuff usually did it. I left him standing there and ran back to get the pickup and trailer then took off after John, Roy, and forty-one head running away.

The boys finally passed 'em got in front of 'em and turned 'em to the north at the next cross dirt road. Eighteen head fell or jumped into a concrete ditch full of water. Roy followed the rest still going north and came to the New River bank and over they went, down to the river bottom. He let them go 'cause we knew where they were. Then he came back to help John and I and the 18 in the canal. They could not get out and were heading down stream to an under the road culvert pipe. A culvert allows the water to go under another road and up on the other side. John started roping them, starting with the furthest one downstream. He would drag one out and I would jump on him before he could get up, take the rope off and let him go on down to the river bottom. John would rope another and drag him out and I would take the rope off, and he would go again. All the time, they were getting closer to that under road culvert. We got five head out and thirteen head disappeared under the water. We rode across the road to see if they would surface and sure enough all 13 popped up. Five head had drowned. Eight head were still alive. John continued to rope those eight head and pull them out of the ditch. As he had pulled them out, Roy would send them on their way down to the river bottom. We finished pulling the dead ones out and loaded them in my trailer. We went back and picked up *Tonka*, he was still standing in the same spot where I had left him. We quickly checked the pasture with the herd in it. They had settled down and were eating good and some were walking along the fence line checking it out. Once in a while to their sudden surprise, it was still hot.

We were all worn out, especially old *Cannon*, after that long run to catch the runaways, passing them and getting them to turn to the north, and then pulling out 18 head from the canal. We dropped off the five dead calves at the Mellowland Feed lot on their dead pile and went on home for dinner, shower, and a good night's sleep. A rest we all deserve.

We went back in the morning to check the other fields to make sure all was well and then to the river looking for the calves lost in the river bottom. We had five hands this morning, John, Roy, Mike, Earl and I. Earl wanted to go and so he saddled *Tonka Jr* and I got on another horse I had named *Big John*. He was a cow horse, strong and would do anything you ask of him. I let *Tonka* rest for a couple of days. We figured this ride shouldn't be too hard on man or beast. We were just going to ride through the toolies and arrow weeds. They were thick, tall and a little difficult on the horse working their way through them while we're looking hopefully to see a steer lost in them. Mike and I were on one side of the river and John, Roy, and Earl spread out on the banks on the other side of the river. I was walking along on *Big John* and came out to a clearing.

We were close to the river edge, when all of a sudden, my horse sunk up to the saddle. *Big John* began to lunge and the more he did, the more he would go down in the quicksand. Now he started to lean over on his left side which made him lay on my leg. I was trapped along with *Big John*. I got him quieted down and quit lunging and I began to holler for help. Mike heard me and came back to me. He had been way up ahead. When he arrived, I told him to stay back. "Don't get too close to me." I didn't want him to get caught in the same trap. I told him to throw me a rope and get me out. *Forget my horse for now.* I didn't know how deep the sand and mud was, and I certainly didn't want to go down with *Big John*. Mike threw me a rope. I put it around under my arms. Mike dallied his end around his saddle horn and pulled me from my horse. *Boy, oh boy!* Was that a good feeling standing on solid ground, even though I was smelly and a mess in that black mud. By then the other three hands arrived. We all started wondering how to get *Big John* out. I decided to lie down on the top of the mud and sand. Leave my feet on the bank, where the boys could hold my legs. I told them I would dig down and untie my latigo strap, tie a rope to the D-Ring on the cinch and one rope on my saddle horn then dally the end to another horse and pull. When my saddle comes off, it would pull the rope that I had tied to the D-Ring on the cinch around my horse's waist. All this time, Mike was holding *Big John's* head up, so he could breathe by the reins on his bridle. We put two ropes around his neck and the one around his waist to another horse. So the three horses began to pull and Big John started lunging again, moving towards solid ground. The men would relax their pull and let him get some air and then go at it again, each time making a little more progress towards hard ground. By the fourth pull, *Big John* could get his front feet on a little solid ground and began to help the horses pulling him out. The final pull got him out on solid ground. He just laid there making awful sounds that I had never heard a horse make. He was shaking all over his body. We all figured he was in shock. After a few minutes, we finally got him up on his feet, still shaking. While he was standing there, gathering himself to some kind of normality, I took my saddle and blanket off and walked up to a cement canal that had running water in it. I threw my saddle and blanket in and jumped in myself. I gave everything a good wash job including myself. I loaded up the horses and the hands, and went home. John Taylor went to check the water and fence on his other herds again. We got home; we unloaded my horses, put them in their pens and fed them. I did put *Big John* on the wash rack first. I got him all cleaned up and gave him some hay and grain. Poor old *Big John* was never quite the same horse after that ordeal.

We went back again to New River until we finally found all but one calf, and come to find out, he had left the river bottom and made his way down the road to the Mellowland Feed lot. They recognized the brand and called John to come get him. Thirty days after the wreck we had found them all. There was plenty of grass and water down in the river bed to sustain them.

Marilyn's Rodeos

This day we were coming out of Bob Lemon's alfalfa pasture, heading west on Cole Rd towards Highway 111. At that intersection, there is a traffic light there today, but not when all this happened. It hadn't been installed yet. John called the highway patrol to come stop traffic for us, which they would do when we would call them. Our plan was to get the herd moving fast. Hopefully, they would shoot straight across the freeway. However the highway patrol didn't show up that day.   All steers came out just fine, so we left Marilyn behind alone on the drag that day because we would need all cowboys up front to keep them going straight and fast to cross Highway 111. About 300 yards into the move out of the pasture something spooked them and they all turned around and started back to the field. Marilyn and *Bucko* were fighting 'em to turn 'em back. So she started running to get ahead of them to try and shut them off at the gate.

She told me, "I thought the only way I could get around these leaders was to run up that steep canal bank." That was soft silt. Halfway up the bank, *Bucko's* front legs went down deep in the silt and tripped him. Both of 'em went end over end which threw Marilyn over his head and she landed on her back on top of the canal bank.

She said, "All I could think of to do was to roll over on my knees start prayin'. I covered my head with both my arms expecting the worse." I started back to her. I was thinking she will surely be injured with a lot of hurt, if she would even survive. I could see the steers going all around her, the dust was so thick, I figured she must be flat down and trampled. My heart was in my throat. When I got to where I thought she was, all of a sudden I saw her stand up, grinning from ear to ear and started dusting herself off.

She said, "Boy I sure thought this was it." She assured me she was alright. She said she could see them through the dust. The cattle were going around both sides of her. All the steers went back into the field and by now all the hands had arrived. I went and got *Bucko* and took him back to Marilyn. She got up on him and we all started all over again, round them up and move them out the gate again, still moving fast down Cole Rd. I stayed on the drag with Marilyn. We kept them pushed up against the hands up front, not giving them a chance to turn back. We got to 111, still no highway patrol, so John took his hat off and flagged the traffic down. The traffic was good and patient with us. We got across the freeway perfectly and to the gate on the left. The pasture was where Wal-Mart and all those businesses are today, on the southeast corner of the acreage. Man, oh man. Two moves in the same day in the same field, lunch time at the De Anza coffee shop.

While we were having lunch, we were all talking and laughing about Marilyn's wrecks that could have really been a bad situation, but the Lord had his hand on her no doubt. We all were remembering Marilyn at the intersection at Cole Road when she had another wreck on a different move. She was blocking a hole, keeping the herd going straight. One steer got out of sorts, so she gave *Bucko* a little spur pressure to move the steer back. When she did, she got her spur stuck in the rear cinch. Now you already know what happened. *Bucko* dumped her on her face at the famous intersection of 111 and Cole Rd. Old *Bucko* did not run off this time. He just stood there turned and was looking at her, probably wondering what happened. She got back on him and helped us finish the move.

Every time we pass that intersection even today, I ask her, "Remember that spot right there, honey."

She always replies, "I sure do." We finished our lunch and went home.

We will always remember Cole Road and Marilyn, poor Marilyn. Another time we had a herd alongside the All American Canal. One bovine moved down in the toolies, so she went down in there to drive him out. We figured the toolies must have jabbed *Bucko* in the flanks, and apparently he did his thing in there because he and the steer came out but no Marilyn. John and I loped over where the animals came out. Benny Derrick caught her horse; we got off of our horses and started looking for her. All we could hear was some moaning. We were pushing the toolies around looking for her and all of a sudden there she was flat on her back. We checked her out and she seemed to be okay so we got her up on her feet. She said she felt fine. I guess it just knocked the wind out of her. She got back on old *Bucko* and we finished the drive. Now, we know why the notch in *Bucko's* ear.

While I am writing about Marilyn I might as well tell all. In another event, we had just moved the herd from one pasture, just across the fence to the next pasture. All was well and we made the move easy. We all were just sitting there on our horses while our fence builder was putting back up the fence. He was stretching the wire with a come-along to close the hole. When the wire snapped it sounded like a 30-30 rifle shot. *Guess what happened next.* Old *Bucko*, broke in half swallowed his head and put on a rodeo for us. Marilyn was going with him pretty good, but she finally lost the battle and off she went. She was always very lucky up till now with no broken bones, however this time her pride was hurt more than her body. She had just had a shampoo and her hair set when she hit the ground. She landed in fresh cow manure. Just think what that looked like and smelled like. The side of her face and hair was all green. Of course, first thing she did was run her hand through her hair which spread the manure all through her hair.

I asked her, "Honey, could you ride home in the horse trailer with the horses?", but that suggestion didn't fly. So we found some rags, cleaned her up the best we could, and took her home to finish the job. A lot of people would ask me, why I didn't let her ride *Tonka* and I ride *Bucko*.

I would tell 'em, "Oh no! That horse is too wild for me." The truth is she wouldn't trade him with me.

She said, "That's my horse, I love to ride him. He is so smooth and comfortable to ride except for those funny things he does once in a while, but even that's exciting about him, not knowing when that is going to happen."

I'll tell you about one more wreck and no doubt it was the worst ever of all her rodeos. We were moving down Farnsworth Rd and she was riding *Tonka Jr.* that day. We were going past the old Pavo Dairy, so she was moving up to block a hole to keep 'em from going in the dairy yard. On her way to close that hole, there was a small irrigation ditch that had grass grown over it. She and *Jr.* didn't notice it, but *Jr.* saw it was a ditch at the last second, and swung his body to the left. He lost his balance and went upside down on top of Marilyn with all four legs straight up in the air. Thank the Lord there was only about a foot of water in the ditch. She was struggling to keep her head above the water while *Jr.* was struggling to try to get to his feet. John, Maurice and Benny saw what happened and ran to get there to help her. They grabbed *Jr.'s reins* and started to pull. Somehow, *Jr.* got over on his side where he could get his front feet traction and began to climb out. Both hind legs were digging for traction and one leg slipped back and hit Marilyn on her right ear, his hoof cut her ear in half, but he finally got out. The boys got Marilyn out, checked her out and put a rag on her ear to stop the bleeding. We finished the move, and then took her to the emergency room to put a couple of stitches in her ear. I've often thought what she would look like today if that hoof had been over three inches and had hit her in the face. Of course, she blamed *Tonka Jr.*

"See I didn't have my horse *Bucko!*" was the first thing out of her mouth. "Man gimme back my horse." It did leave a permanent indentation on the front of her left thigh where the saddle horn was punched into her leg from the weight of *Jr.* and all his struggling. Tough gal I married as well as still pretty.

Sugar Beets Pasture

One summer, my brother Stan and his wife, Viv were coming through town on their way east. They stayed a few days with us. It was always good to have them visit with us, but better when we could hook up our fifth wheel RV and head out with them to places unknown. Viv was the greatest tour guide.

The first afternoon they were here, Johnny and I had to check a few head that we were pasturing on sugar beet tops. The beet digger would go through the field and cut off the beet top with the green foliage on it, leaving the tops in the field. After the digger went through the field, we would put a herd in the field for them to eat. The first time the cattle went on the beet tops, they did not know what they were, so they just walked the field for a day or so looking for something green to eat. Once they ate one of those sugar beet tops, they loved them and would gain three to four pounds a day. That of course, is what John wanted. The problem with pasturing beet tops is they sometimes would swallow one that was too big and it would get stuck in their throat. Now, they couldn't eat or drink. They would always go to a water tank to try to wash it down. They would stand there drinking and the water would come back out through their nose. When this would happen, we would ride in the field, sneak up on the steer, throw a loop on his head, and pull him out to a clearing. The other hand would rope his hind legs and pull him down on his side. Then the header would move up and give the steer some slack as we always did. Take the loop off his head and put it on his front legs snap the rope at your horse and he would back up holding the steer tight. We put the rope around his front feet, so the rope wouldn't choke anymore than he already was. We carried about a two inch rubber hose on the back of our saddles. We would put a knee on his neck, take the hose, open his mouth and start the hose down his throat until we hit the stuck beet. Then bump it with a little pressure and push it right on down to his stomach. The gas that builds up in his stomach explodes out the end of that hose.

Now, Brother Stan wanted to come along that day, so I saddled *Bucko* that day for him and away we went to check the fields. The first field we went to, there was a steer at the drinker all choked up. So, Johnny roped him by the head, pulled him away from the drinker and I roped his heels. We stretched him out and Johnny gave him some slack. He got off of *Cannon*, took the loop off of the steer's head and put it around his front legs. He snapped his rope and *Cannon* backed up to hold him tight. He took the hose off of his saddle and started the procedure. I told Johnny, that I was going to let Stan blow on the end of the hose instead of me and that I'll just stay on my horse and keep the rope tight. John caught my evil thought, so I said to Stan, "Get off *Bucko* and go help John and he will tell you what to do." So Stan got off, just dropped his reigns and old *Buck* just stood there. Stan walked over to John and he told him, "When I tell you Stan, blow on the end of that hose." Stan got in position to do the blowing.

John pushed the beet down the throat of that steer and then pushed Stan out of the way at the same time, and spared my brother a horrible mess all over himself. When that gas and junk comes out of that steer through the hose, it stinks. *Wow!* After a big laugh and calming Stan down, John let the steer up and got on his horse. Now Stan was a big man, so when he went to get back on *Bucko*, his weight pulled *Bucko* sideways towards him. When he threw his legs over *Bucko's* back, he went clear over him and landed hard flat on his back on the ground. One more big laugh. We finally got him up on his horse, and then went looking for another patient. We found nothing more on that field, so we went on to another field of sugar beets looking for more chokes. Only one that day.

We Took No Pictures

In all of the years of wrangling cattle, we didn't take any pictures which would have been impossible, I think. I can't see chasing a maverick to rope him and trying to take a picture of the action at the same time. However, people going by on the road took many, many pictures. Some folks we know passing by, would take pictures occasionally, and they would give me a print of what they had taken while passing by. Some would meet at a field to see the action.

One day we were moving a herd from pasture to corral so we could ship them by cattle truck to a distant pasture. It was too far to drive them on horseback. When they travel from field to field, Johnny figured a three percent shrink from the walking the distance. We were going east down Highway 98 and one old wild steer at the end of the herd decided he wanted to go back to the field he came out of. The girls bringing up the drag couldn't turn him, so they let him go. One of the hands working the side of the herd saw him run off and so he took off after him. John and I saw a car stop in the middle of the road and a young man got out and was standing in the road waiting for that angry maverick to get to him. John and I started laughing because that fella was about to meet that steer head on. We were assuming he would get knocked flat on his back, but the next time we looked back. The steer was down on the pavement and the guy had his knee on the steer's neck and his front leg bent back to where he couldn't get up. When Maurice got there, he put a loop on his neck and the guy let him up and Maurice followed him on a gallop to the herd, dropped his rope and let it drag behind him to the corral and there, we could get it off.

We found out who bulldogged the steer in the middle of the highway. It was Ricky Johnson, one of Dickie Johnson's sons. Now Ricky is a real cowboy and knew exactly what he was doing when he tangled with that bovine. We were laughing because we thought it was just a traveler going to get his clock cleaned. All of the cattle were in the corral and the trucks finally arrived, got in place at the end of the chute and ready to load. The driver would tell us how many head he wanted in the section of the truck he was loading.

Two of us in the pen, would count out the number he would ask for and would begin to crowd them up the ramp into the truck. One old, angry bovine didn't want to go up the chute. He turned and charged *Tonka* and hit him in his left front shoulder and upside down he went with me on the ground alongside of him. We both scrambled to our feet and I got back on him, and finished loading all of them. Then off to the pasture where we were sending the herd to. We had a portable chute for loading and unloading livestock that we could pull behind our pickups. Since this herd were used to being out on pasture, they just walked off the truck and started eating, nothing like the new steers that have never been out on pasture. Both *Tonka* and I were covered pretty well with cow manure from our fall, got most of it off before we got in the truck. When we got home, Marilyn made me undress outside on the patio and then come in the house in my shorts, and head straight for the shower.

The Loss of Our Friends

After all the herds were in the feed lots for the summer, they were never to return to pasture grazing again. Marilyn and I took off on our vacation to the Northwest where we've been going for the last few years. Mainly, we've been going to Corbett, Oregon on the scenic highway, 20 miles upriver from Portland on the Columbia River. Man, now that's gorgeous country. If you have never been there, you should make plans for a vacation in the Northwest at least once in your lifetime. Put it on your bucket list.

This year we met Stan and Viv, my brother and sister-in-law, Bob Kirby, a cousin, and his wife, Dorothy. All pulling our R.V.'s we left for Victoria, Canada. We arrived in Port Angeles, Washington, where we caught a ferry boat to cross over to Victoria, a beautiful city in Canada. When we got back to Corbett from our trip to Canada, I had a phone call from home that *Tonka* and *Tonka Jr.*, *Dusty* and *Samantha* got out of the pasture about 1:30AM, they went down the road to John's corral, ate their fill of hay, then *Tonka* and *Tonka Jr* went out on the southbound lanes of Clark Rd, where they were standing there side by side and a fast moving pickup truck driven by a young man who was a dear friend of ours as well as his whole family hit them and killed them instantly. Thank goodness it was quick and no suffering. We were also thankful, this young man wasn't hurt, but it totaled out his truck. It wasn't his fault. It was a very dark night and both horses were almost black in color. He really felt bad because the horses belonged to me. Bless his heart, he was so apologetic. *Dusty* would always check the gate latches two or three times daily on the gates, he had figured out how to use his nose to unlock the pasture gates, so I put snaps on each gate, so they wouldn't open. A friend brought his girlfriend out to see the horses, took the snap off and went in the pasture to pet them. When they left the pasture, they left the snap off the gate latches. It was still lying on the ground when we got home from Oregon. Old *Dusty* found the gate with no snap, nosed up the latch and set them all free, and out they ran. From that time on, I put padlocks on each gate to the pastures.

Now *Dusty* stayed at John's haystack. *Samanatha* was standing on the side of the road by *Tonka* and *Jr*. When the truck hit them, it knocked them into *Samantha*. It really banged her up and she could hardly walk. But she recovered and was back in our six pony hitch. Well that brought to a close of my horses that were totally a big part of my life, if ever two animals went to heaven, those two did. The bible tells us that God owns all the cattle on a thousand hills. So when I get there, I'll need old *Tonka* and Marilyn will need *Jr.* to herd all those cattle like we did here on Earth with John Taylor. I found a little quarter horse in El Centro for sale. He was 14.2 hands tall, 950 pounds; a four year old and green broke. I bought him and took him home and began to train him to rope. He learned quick and I really enjoyed working with him. Every morning, when I would first get on him, it was always a rodeo. After a couple of humps he was okay for the rest of the day. I liked him because he was so small. He was easy to get on now that I'm getting old, and it don't hurt so bad when you fall off. My brother went back to Montrose, Colorado and found me a good horse for sale. I told him to buy him if you think he is as good as you say he is, and then bring him to El Centro for me. Stan showed up in about two weeks with the horse. He was a beautiful palomino with dapple spots all over him. So that's why I named him Freckles. So, now I was back in the horse business and ready to go back to work for John Taylor for the new pasture season starting in October. We always took all herds in the feed lots in August and the new calves out in October. Hang on folks; here we go again for new adventures. We don't know what's in store for us this coming year, but no doubt, it will be exciting and fun.

The Lettuce Patch

We were moving five hundred head west on McCabe Rd. Uncle Wyatt and Aunt Frances would come out to the valley and spend the winter with us to get out of the cold snow from Montrose, Colorado. They would park their trailer out at the barn. I called it "pay-back time". They were one of the aunts and uncles that I would spend the summer with in Montrose as a kid. So I told them it was get even time. The old outhouse that is on display at the mine, seen at the Broken Spoke Golf Course was at my barn area for their convenience.

We always called my uncle, "Willie." He was a real cowboy all his life and he loved to herd cattle up in the mountains of Colorado, and of course with John Taylor and his crew when they were here in El Centro.

On this day we had our herd heading for McCabe Cattle Company on LaBrucherie Road. Willie and I were the only two hands up front leading the way that day. The herd was moving faster than usual and we had to get them slowed down before we got to the feed yard because we had to make a right hand turn and going as fast as they were going, we knew it was going to be a difficult turn with only two cowboys. The turn was coming up fast and we certainly were going to have to have more help up front to make that right angle turn in just a couple of minutes. I saw John coming as quickly as he could but I knew he wasn't going to make it in time to help us.

We got to the corner and Uncle Willie turned right and took the lead and I was bumping them to him as hard as I could go but the cattle were coming so fast and there were so many that they got away from me and started running on both sides of me and *Tonka*. I was hollerin' and fightin' the best I could. Finally, John and Maurice arrived and the cattle were out into a lettuce field. Usually I would take after the leader to get them to turn, but in this case there were no leaders. There was just one big herd fanning out in the corner of the lettuce field.

By now the other hands arrived so all of us took off around them in the lettuce field to circle and stop them and to get 'em started back out of the field. We were all running wide open across field rows. *Now if you want something to make you pucker up in the saddle, try running your horse across lettuce furrows.* A race horse sometimes will break a leg running on perfect dirt and that was going through my mind while *Tonka* was jumping furrows and lettuce heads. Thank the Lord he was very sure-footed and had big leg bones. We all got them circled and stopped their running. We let them settle down and then we began to push them out of the field, north and LaBrucherie Road and into McCabe feed lot at last.

The insurance company had John fence off about three acres of lettuce that he had damaged. Then when the good lettuce was sold the market value was assessed and John's insurance company settled with the farmer for $25,000.00 dollars. That's a good example as to why it was so important for John to carry insurance.

A Wild West Lunch

Fifteen miles out of town, there was an old country schoolhouse known as Mount Signal School. Today, it is a restaurant. After we would make our moves from one pasture to another one somewhere out in that area, we all would go to the Mount Signal Cafe for a great Mexican lunch.

One cowboy that was helping us out that day was a wild dude, but an excellent cowboy and as funny as a crutch. When he talked, he had a horrible stuttering problem and you couldn't understand him, but he could talk by singing. Whenever he would try to tell us something, we would always say, "Jim, sing what you're tryin' to say now." Jimmy Galbreath could sing what he was trying to say, but couldn't speak it without stuttering. Anyway, Jimmy was a good guy and we always had a lot fun with him whenever he would help us on a move. One day, all the men were having lunch. Jimmy finished his lunch first and all of the sudden disappeared. Now the Mount Signal Cafe had double front doors and all of the sudden they flew open and in rode Jimmy on his horse. Customers began to scatter and scramble, upsetting chairs and tables. Sandra, the owner was screaming, "Get out! Get out!"

Jimmy looked like John Wayne in an old western bar fight. We got him and his horse out of the cafe and cleaned up the mess. We got Sandra settled down and then left to move another herd, laughing all the way to the next field. That's Jimmy! You never knew what he was going to do when he was with us. *Now, that was really fun.*

A Steer Guest for Dinner

The crew all met at John's Corrals at about 8:00am, we loaded up the horses and started south down on to Clark Rd down into the New River bottom. Then we turned right on Kubler Road about three miles to the field where our herd was at. That herd, we were moving in to John Kubler's Feed Lot. We started the same procedure, three hands in the field and fanning out to the rear of the field to begin rounding them up, pushing them towards the gate. They were moving good and out the gate, smooth as silk, with no problem. Thus far, we were moving east now on Kubler Road.

By the time we got to Farrell Rd, which was a mile from the feed lot, they began to get a little tired and hot. It was a very warm day and we probably should have left a little earlier that morning. We knew it was going to be a hot day, but there we were. Things were getting ready to happen, but we had no idea, how bad it was going to get. Well, here we go, so you always wanted to be a cowboy, huh?!!

One old Brahma steer broke away from the tail end of the herd and started back towards the field that we had come from. Grandpa Burl took off after him on his good old steed, *Dusty*, but that steer was giving him a good foot race. The steer was getting real hot, no doubt. When they do that, they go crazy and on the fight. It came to Farrall Road, turned south and headed straight for John Kubler's house. It went through the plants and shrubbery surrounding John's patio with Burl right on his tail. Up on his patio, the steer saw his own image in the sliding glass door and charged it full force. He hit that door and went right on through it. John's son ran to get out of the room and shut the hall door behind him, so that mad bovine could not go down the hall. Thank the Lord for that. That mad old steer went wild in that room, tearing up everything in his way. What was a beautiful den, now was totally destroyed, blood from bad cuts on him and manure all over everything. The hands finally got him back out the door, got a rope on him, dragged him through the shrubbery, got behind him with the rope around his neck and followed behind him. You can guide a steer by running behind him holding the rope and when he wanders the wrong direction, you can turn him back to go straight ahead with your horse, or slow him down if he is going too fast by dallying your rope around the saddle horn. Grandpa did a good job making him run straight ahead all the way down the hill to Kubler's Feed lot.

Now John attends the same church that all of us attend. I remind him occasionally at church and we all have a good laugh and I say, "Hey Johnny, remember when we remodeled your den?"

John Taylor called his insurance company and they sent out an adjuster. Poor guy couldn't believe what had happened to that room. It looked like a bad train wreck, but they put it all back together, exactly the way the Kubler's wanted it done. The steer got his cuts and bruises all patched up. We probably ate the sucker in a hamburger later that year. Thank the Lord for some good people like John Kubler. He, being a cattle man, knows that strange things can happen when dealing with bovine.

Lost and Found Horses

One morning, the hands met at John's Corral early. We were going to Allied Feed Lot down towards Calexico to take a herd out to pasture. When we arrived at the yard, we all got out of the truck and to our surprise; there was no trailer and no horse. John had backed up his truck to the trailer hitch and forgot to make the hitch while we were loading horses and talking to each other. We all got in and didn't know John hadn't hooked up. So off we go talking, laughing, and joking with each other.

We realized what had happened and wanted to get out of there as soon as we could because of the humiliation of laughter. So John and I jumped in the pickup and left the others there and we went back to get the horses, shaking our heads and laughing at what a dumb thing to do. When we pulled in the barn yard, there sat the trailer with five horses standing in it. They were probably wondering what was going on, too. With more shaking our heads, we wondered how in the world we could have done such a thing, let alone drive ten miles and not realize the trailer wasn't back there. So we hooked up, took off for the Allied Feed lot and when we got there, we were met by a group of cowboys laughing and pointing at us.

We unloaded the horses cinched up our saddles and counted out the steers, which we always did when we take them in a yard and when we take them out. Always count in and out, so we knew what we put in and the count should always be the same going back out. The way we would count, it was usually John and I doing the counting. We could put all five hundred or whatever in an alley and then the boys would push them in single file passed us sitting on our horses. We would count five at a time silently. If for some reason, they would get to coming faster than a single file we moved our horses in and shut them off. When they would settle down, we let them start coming by us again. Then we would continue our counting, five at a time. When we got our count, John's figures and my figures would match and that would match with the feed lot count. We would work our way to the front of the herd whichever end of the alley we would be going out.

When we were working our way through the crowded alley, I noticed five head of steers in one pen, dead with their feet up in the air. I asked one of the feed lot hands, "What happened to those five" and as I rode by he said, "They got into the oleander plants," which are deadly to animals. An animal won't eat them on purpose, but he said a few leaves got into their hay, and of course they ate them not knowing they were there in the hay. Too bad, but those things happen.

Well, we finally got them going down the road. Just before we got to the field we had a little wreck, but we finally got them into the field that we wanted. All except one that had broken his front leg below his knee. So we cut him out of the herd, so we could load him in the trailer and take him back to the feed lot for care. Before John could rope him, he got down in a dry concrete ditch. So I got off my horse, jumped down in the ditch to move him down to a place where he could get out.

John was on his horse, walking along beside him with his rope ready to catch him. For some reason, that bovine turned and started running down in the bottom of that concrete ditch as hard as he could run, coming straight for me. I turned and was making tracks and that sucker was mad and in pain and was right on my fanny. When a steer gets hurt or too hot, they always get mad and on to fight. He was just about to nail me when I heard John's rope whirling around and around over his head and then he threw his loop at the steer's head and every step I was making I was prayin', "Lord, don't let him miss this time or I'm gonna have a lot of hurt on me." I heard John jerk his slack and dally around his saddle horn. He just kept pulling the steer out of the ditch. One of the hands brought the trailer up and John pulled him in the trailer up front where we could shut the center gate on him so he couldn't move that much. To help him with his pain of the leg flopping around, we took him back to the feed lot and gave him to their men to take care of. We went back to pick up the horses and the other boys and then cut for Camacho's for our late lunch.

Tom and Jerry Save the Day

John always had most of his herds in the south land of Imperial Valley around the Highway 98 area. He had what we called dry lots to put the cattle in when it would rain. If we did not have a dry lot close by, then we would have to drive them in the rain to the nearest feed lot. During the rainy season, we would have to use all hands available. Cattle don't like to move in stormy weather. We would have to go to each field and round up each herd in their pasture and move them to one of our dry lots or to the nearest feed yard. If we didn't get them off the pasture with the rain soaking the ground, they would walk restlessly and trample the alfalfa or grass into the mud and totally destroy the field. A dry lot was nothing but dirt fenced in with drinkers at one end of it for water. We would haul hay to them until the pastures were dry and then take them back to their fields.

Each herd had to have its own dry lot or feed yard to go to, so we wouldn't get the brands mixed up with each other. Sometimes, it would involve a few-mile move to find a dry lot or a feed yard in the wind and rain. Thank the Lord; we seemed to have plenty of cowboys to help. Seasoned or rookies, anybody that could ride a horse was welcome. The cattle were always squirrelly to move in wind and rain and would want to go their own direction rather than follow the herd. It was very tiring for the cowboys and their horses, running in the mud, trying to keep them all bunched together till we could get them to the dry lot or feed yard.

One lot we moved into was solid mud. After 500 head walking back and forth, bog clear up to their knees, we started into the lot with a wagon loaded with 30 bales of hay. We were using a four-wheel drive tractor, and pulled the load about a hundred feet in the mud when the wagon buried itself to the axles. Now, the tractor couldn't get traction, it just sat there and spun all four wheels. I told John to take me home and I'll get my Clydesdale team and I'll pull that wagon to the end of the lot where we needed to feed the hay. So, home I go. I threw on the old work harness up on the big boys and loaded them in the trailer and off we went to pull the wagon loaded with hay, stuck in the mud, buried up to the axles.

I unloaded the big guys, walking behind them, and drove them out to the wagon slowly to keep my boots from pulling off in the mud. I backed them up to the wagon, hooked them up to it and I climbed up on the top bale of hay. John said, 'Kirb, I don't think they can pull it out of there." *Tom* was my lead horse, so I asked for *Tom* and when *Jerry* hears that, he knows what it means. They both hit the collars at the same time and the wagon began to move. I made about a fifty foot pull and I stopped to let them get their breath. It was a beautiful sight to see. They had shoes on with corks and their feet went down to hard ground, where they could get traction, whereas the tractor wheels would just spin in the mud. I let them rest a minute and asked for *Tom* and we went for another fifty feet and rested. Their nostrils were flaring, and you could see their breath coming out because it was cold that morning. Their rib cages were going in and out as they would regain their wind and rally some more strength. We did this three times and on the fourth pull, *Big Jerry* lost his footing and down he went on his side. I was talking to him to stay still while I dug in the mud and unbuckled his harness, so he could get to his feet again. The mud was all over his body, under his collar and harness. Both horses were so muddy you couldn't tell they had white legs. I got him hooked back up and made the final pull. We fed the cattle then I loaded the boys and took off for the car wash in El Centro. I took the high pressure hose and began to spray them while they were still in the trailer where they couldn't get away from me. It took me about a half an hour to get the most of it off. I went back to the barn and they had an extra serving of grain. I finished cleaning their harness. It was wonderful to watch all that power, when you hook 4000 pounds of muscle to something. Something is going to move or break.

The Different Cattle That We Received

Most of our cattle were crossbreeds, with Brahma crossed with Angus or Hereford breeds. Now, Hereford or Angus straight breed can't do well in the heat, but crossbreeding with the Brahma breed, they can lie down in the sun and gain weight. The Brahma breed is a lot wilder than the Hereford and the Angus, and a little more trouble to care of. We did have a herd of straight Angus one time that were good calves to take care of, but when it started getting hot we took them into the feed lot.

Almost all of our crossbreeds came to us from Oklahoma and Texas. Sometimes we would get a load of steers out of Mexico. They were always so docile and it seemed they could eat weeds and gain weight. One time we got a shipment of calves from the swamps of Florida. You talk about wild. Those calves didn't know what a human or a horse was. All they knew was swamps, snakes, and alligators. A lot of them had no tails or were missing an ear; possibly a good lunch for an alligator.

These calves were hard to catch if you had to doctor one. They would run with their tails straight in the air and I mean *run*. Sometimes, we had to use one cowboy to run them down and get them tired and then a fresh cowboy would move in on the chase. The next hand would then be getting him tired when the third hand would move in and make an easy catch. We only had this Florida herd one time. Thank the Lord for that. I told John, "You order another load of those calves and I quit!"

Once in a while, we would be on the ground working on a drinker and a steer would walk out of the group come up to us while we were working and rub his head against us. We would then realize at once, that this steer was raised by some kid that had raised him for a fair or something. We would rub him all over his back and head and when we got back on our horse it would usually follow us back to the gate balling. You couldn't help but feel a little sorry for the rascal, because he was missing his friend, whoever raised him, and the next time they would meet would possibly be on a dinner plate.

The Last Cattle Drive

This morning the phone rang and it was John. He said, "Kirby saddle up your horse. Let's go a little earlier this morning." So, I saddled up *Slick* and rode down the road to John's house. We were going to make our last drive today. I had walked down the lane with a hot cup of coffee, no breakfast and mixed emotions. I was glad it was the last move for the summer, but hated the thought that it was our last move, forever. I did my chores, but not many were left. I threw a little scratch for the chickens. *Jerry* was already gone *Arnie* and *Barnie* also gone, the pigs were gone, roping calves gone, the chickens were all turned out and running wild now. *Dugan Duck* and *Turkey Lurkey* and all our cats and along with our little dog, *Dixie*, of 17 years; gone, all gone.

I started thinking while I was brushing down *Slick* while he was eating his grain. *Where did those 24 years go?* I won't only miss *Slick* and the cattle, but the fellowship with some great friends and professional cowboys, and of course teasing our wives, Vera and Marilyn, who were always on the dusty end of the drive. Bless their hearts. They never complained after the one stampede that got away from them when they wanted to take the lead that one time. I got *Slick* all brushed and saddled and started down the lane. As soon as I swung my leg over his back and took a deep seat in my saddle, we got the two jumps out of the way. I walked over to John. I usually loped over, but this morning I just wanted this day to last a little longer than usual. When I got to John's Corral, the crew for the day was all there ready to go. John, Maurice, Mike and now, me. Four of us. There wasn't quite 500 head and they had been moved many, many times before, so John figured, the four hands could do it with no trouble. We got to the field about four miles west on McCabe Road. It was to be a straight shot east to the McCabe Cattle Co. The only turn we had was a left turn on LaBrucherie to the McCabe Cattle yard. The herd came out of the field like they were supposed to, and moved along very well, but slow. Little did they know it was their last move too. I wanted to move slow to make it last. I kept thinking maybe we can have a wreck at the bridge coming up at the corner of McCabe and Austin, just one last wreck, please. But we arrived at the bridge and the darned beasts just went across that bridge, perfectly. *Oh, shoot!*, I said to myself, *Maybe later on down the road*, but our last wreck never came. It was absolutely a perfect move, slow and quiet, not one steer wandered off of the trail. We got to McCabe, made a perfect left turn to the front gate of the feed yard.

We bent the leaders into the first lane, made our count which was perfect, and shook hands with the feed lot hands. We told them all "goodbye" and thanks for all their help over the years. I got a ride back to the field to get the trailer. I came back to pick up the men and horses, and go on home for the last time. We unloaded our horses and told each other goodbye, with a firm handshake and a few hugs. Maurice and Mike left and I just stood there holding *Slick's* reigns and John was holding *Poco's*. We both leaned up against his truck and looked at each other for a few seconds.

I broke the silence and spoke first, "Johnny, I want to thank you so much, for 24 of the happiest years of my life without questions."

"Yes Kirby, it was a good time, and I want to thank you and Marilyn for all your years helping and of course, our friendship." We both had tears in our eyes, because his wrangling years were over.

I said, "Johnny, what are you gonna do with *Poco*?" He looked at his watch and said a guy will be here in about an hour to pick him up. I said, "What?!"

"Yep. Kirby, I rode horses for 40 years, only because it was my business to, and I'll never get on another one for the rest of my life.", and he didn't, either.

I said, "John you need something you can curry down, and saddle him up for your grandkids to ride."

"No!" He said, "A horse was strictly business for me and not pleasure."

I said, "What about your saddle?"

He said, "It goes, too." I just shook my head, grabbed him and gave him a big hug, shook his hand and looked him straight in the eye, "I love you, Johnny," I said. "John, you will ride again and look after cattle, and old *Cannon* or *Poco* will be there for you. *Tonka* and I will be there to help you, and our wives will love to ride the drag then, because there's no dust in heaven. The reason I know this, John because the book of Psalms, 50th chapter, 10th verse says, 'God owns the cattle on a thousand hills and he's gonna need cowboys.' We'll pick you and Vera up for dinner at the Cameo about six."

He said, "Okay Kirb, we'll be ready." I got up on *Slick* and started down the road home. I just walked along slow, thinking about all those years. *Where did they go, where did they go?* How fast they went by. When I turned down McCabe Road towards home, even *Slick* seemed to know it was his last move. He was carrying his head low as I was, too. I thought to myself with a cool breeze at my back and an honest horse between my knees.

I didn't sleep well the last night of the last cattle drive. After we had dinner together, we all went home. When I went to bed and laid my head down on my pillow, I just laid there thinking about all those years with cattle and horses and wondering what's going to be next in my life.

This is Slick after his last cattle drive. He was never rode again. Tom is in the background looking out of the half door of his stall.

PART 2

After 25 Years of Cattle Drives

In 1997, after everything we had was sold, we started spending our summers in Corbett, Oregon. I heard about the Historical Society of Portland. They had a 1903 electric trolley and seven miles of track used only by the trolley. It ran from Lake Oswego to the waterfront of Portland. I looked up their phone number and gave them a call. I told the person on the phone, I would like to work on your trolley. He asked me a little bit about myself. I told him my age, that I was retired, and I just wanted something to do. They asked me to come down to fill out an application, so I did.

They accepted my application on the spot and gave me my workday schedule and hours. They gave me a motorman's hat to wear and told me to wear black pants, a white long sleeve shirt, and a black bow tie. I had two garters that I put around my sleeves up above my elbow. I showed up for my first day and told my boss that I was concerned, "If we get lost or hijacked, what should we do?" He just stared at me for a minute and then it dawned on him. We are on tracks and there was no way we could get lost or hijacked. Then he got a big grin on his face. He gave me a ticket puncher to punch the customer's tickets.

The track ran along the shore of the beautiful Willamette River. I enjoyed interacting with the people and pointing out different points of interests. The museum gave me a book of interesting points to memorize, so I could tell the patrons the answers to their questions immediately. After a few weeks, I finally made motorman. *That was fun!* The trolley had a bell that you operated with your foot at intersections and I would really get after that bell. *Ding! Ding! Ding! Ding! Ding!* Then I would call out the name of the street, "Fifth Avenue!" loud and clear!

Here I am driving a 1903 trolley from Lake Oswego to the waterfront in Portland, Oregon for the Historical Society.

The Trip of a Lifetime

It was September 1, 1979 and the cattle were all in the yards until October. So, Stan, Vivian, Marilyn and I took off from El Centro angling Northeast across the country heading for Banger, Maine. We arrived in Maine on October 1st. I wouldn't be back to work cattle with Johnny Taylor until the 1st of December. He had plenty of wranglers to help him get ready for the 1979 season. We had just buried my favorite uncle, Stan Potter who was a major influence in my life.

It took us 31 days to go that distance because we visited friends and family and historical sites along the way. The first town we hit in Maine was a little country town called Fryeburg. Just inside the city limits was a sign that said "County Fair Horse and Ox Pulling Contest" today. We found a place where we could park two large R.V.'s and went to the fair. It was the first time that I ever tasted French fries with malt vinegar... man what a treat.

We worked our way over to the barn area and went in and found our seats. Outside the barn, we passed by about 10 teams of oxen with their yokes on their necks and a buggy whip in the middle of the yoke. I asked why the whips were leaning up against the yokes and I was told that "that's the way we park 'em." They don't need to tie them up. They have been trained that when that whip was leaning against their yoke then that meant they were tied up and not to move. They drove them by voice commands. "Gee" to the right. "Haw" to the left. "Whoa" to stop and "Clucken" to go. They would hook them with a chain down the middle of the yoke and hook it to a sled called a "stone boat" and add weight to it and then ask their teams to pull it for five minutes. The team that pulled it the farthest in five minutes would win. They could stop the team and let them rest as long as they wanted to, but the clock would still be running. Fascinating!

After the oxen, came the draft horses and the same thing all over again, they pulled for five minutes. The teamster can put his shoulder against his horses rear-end and push him, which I'm sure would help some. They could stop and let them blow, but the clock was still running. On the West Coast, we pull 20 feet and add more weight until they can't pull any more. The one pulling the farthest in the last pull is the winner. After watching this I got so excited that I told myself that I had to have a team of draft horses.

We continued on to Boothbay, Maine where we ate Maine lobster every way they could fix it, including breakfast.... egg omelets with lobster. We stayed there for 3 days and ate lobster, lobster and more lobster.

Next, we headed south to New Hampshire, Massachusetts, Rhode Island, Connecticut, and New York City and hit every interesting place in the city. We stayed in New Jersey and would take the subway into the city every day.

Finally, onto the Amish Country in Lancanster County, Pennsylvania.... a little town called Bird-in-Hand...probably 99% Amish. We found an R.V. Park where my trailer backed up to a fence with a field on the other side that was being tilled with a disc, pulled by five horses abreast, going back and forth, up and down the field. The young man was standing on the evener, driving the hitch and as they walked he would go up and down about 8" as they walked along... a very big "No, No!!" I was taught to never stand in front of the disc like that. If we didn't have a seat to sit on then we had to walk alongside the disc and drive them from there.

I was so fascinated by it that I sat there watching that young man until dusk. He unhitched the horses from the disc and drove the team into the barn, took off their harnesses and then fed them. He then came out and brought 25 head of milk cows into the barn and milked them and then turned them back out to pasture. He then went inside his house...I'm sure to eat dinner.

I got up early the next morning to watch all the activity. I had arranged my chair where I could see what was going to happen. It was still dark when here came this kid with a lantern and gathered the cows again to milk.

They don't have electricity, so I could see their lanterns going back and forth past the windows in the barn. After milking they all went back into the house for breakfast. Then back in the barn to harness horses. Here comes this young man driving his five horses abreast, hitch out to the field, hooked them up to the disc. He got up on the evener again and started doing his bouncing up and down that field, while standing on that evener.

We went to an auction in Bird-in-Hand for farm horse-drawn equipment and buggies. We left the Amish country and headed on south site-seeing different historical sites. We left Stan and Viv in South Carolina and went down to Florida and met Marilyn's Aunt Traudi in Mims, Florida. She showed us the sites…Kennedy Space Center, Cypress Gardens and many other spots. We then received a call from Stan saying they had discovered Jackal Island off the coast of Georgia. He said the seafood was out of this world. So, Marilyn and I took off for Jackal Island and it was as he said. We all would love to go back again. The squirrels were thick and tame. We opened the door of our R.V. and sat down on the floor. Those little rascals would come in and climb up on our laps, so we would feed them peanuts. They would fill their cheeks full of nuts and run out to store them somewhere and back for another load.

We left them and started for California. We drove southwest from Jackal Island and picked up the I-10 and headed for home in El Centro. 10 days later, we were home and I was back in the saddle and glad to be there, my horse between my legs felt so good.

Traveling and visiting historical places in our wonderful country and fond memories we have, but on the back of my horse is home.

We Found Our Hitch

After we returned home from our trip and after being at Freiberg and watching the horse pulling contest with those big draft horses, I listened to their owners calling out commands and pulling their hearts out for him. I told myself I have to have a team and I knew what breed I wanted. I wanted a show team rather than a working team. I wanted to use them to advertise my restaurants in El Centro in the winter and in Colorado in the summer.

I remembered I had met an elderly gentleman by the name of Mr. Don McInnis. He was showing his horses at the Oregon state fair one summer in Salem, while Marilyn and I were vacationing in Corbett, Oregon. I told him I was looking for a team of Clydesdales that were broke the best, and I was wondering if he knew of any for sale. He first suggested I buy a team like his Belgian hitch. I told him I had my heart set on Clydes. So, he thought a minute and said, there was a team of black Clydesdales owned by a feller named, Ike Bay in Hillsboro, Oregon. He looked up his phone number and gave it to me. When I got home in Corbett, I called him to see if he would be interested in selling them. I couldn't believe what he said to me.

"Yes, I had that team and they are just what you are looking for. Their names are *Tom* and *Jerry*, and they are brothers, perfectly matched and broke the best, but I had to sell some horses so they were sold to a feller by the name of Roger Reinhardt in Hinsdale, Montana."

He happened to have his phone number. He gave it to me, so I called Roger when I got home in El Centro. I asked him right out, I hear you have a team of black Clydesdales named *Tom* and *Jerry*. Roger answered, "I sure do.", and I got a shot of adrenaline in the middle of my gut. So, I said would you be in interested in selling them and he said, "You know I think I would because I am changing breeds of horses and they don't match my new hitch of Percherons that I am changing to.

"Wow!" I got another shot of adrenaline in my gut. I replied, "What do you have to have for them." We agreed on a price and then I told him that I'd like to see them first. Roger said, "I'll tell you what, I will put them in a parade in Billings, Montana in September and you can meet me there and see them in action. If you like 'em load 'em up and take 'em home to California".

I said, "That's a good idea." When the time came, Marilyn and I hooked up the horse trailer and cut for Billings. We arrived the day of the parade. We found a place to sit on a curb and watch the parade. It wasn't long until we saw those two big boys coming in their beautiful harness shining in the sun.

When they got up to where we were sitting, I hollered at the driver, "That's got to be *Tom* and *Jerry*!" And the driver hollered back, "You got to be Jack Kirby from California." I was grinnin' from ear to ear.

I replied, "You're right."

Then Roger said, "Meet me at the park about six blocks down the road," which was the end of the parade and strangely enough, that is where we happened to have parked our truck and trailer.

When we got there, Roger had climbed down off of the dray wagon. We made our introductions to each other. While he was standing there on the ground with us, I asked him, are they well broke?

His reply was "They sure are watch this." With no one on the wagon and no one holding the lines, he said to *Tom*, "*Tom*, step up" and the team moved up and then he said "Whoa!" and they stop. He then said back up and they had backed up to where they had started from and again he said "whoa!"

My next remark was "Sold!" Then I asked about the show harness he had on them. I'll take this amount, Roger said. I brought their work harness with me and I'll just throw that in with the deal. I wrote him a check and loaded up the boys and the two harnesses, and started down the road for home. Man, oh man, my dream had come true, what those Clydesdales are going to get Marilyn and me into is a full book in itself. You will hear of some of the events we do during the summer vacation time. The Lord did it again. Just what we had asked for. It's now late October, time to work cattle again with John and Vera.

Tom and Jerry

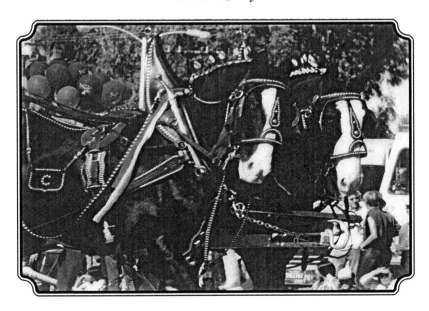

El Centro, California – Tom and Jerry in the Christmas Parade.

So You Wanna Be a Cowboy?

Brawley, California – Tom and Jerry in the Cattle Call Parade. The Grand Marshall is seated next to me, and Marilyn is seated in the wagon.

Yuma, Arizona – The grand entry at the Silver Spur Rodeo. The Marine Base Commander and his family are in the surrey.

Waverly, Iowa Auction

One summer, Marilyn and I were vacationing in Montrose with Stan and Viv. Stan, and one of his very close friends, Norm Natzke, and I decided to go to the Waverly, Iowa's *Fall Horse and Farm* equipment sale. Norm, who was actually an old crony, but a great guy, was also a registered Black Angus cattle dealer. He also raised black Percheron draft horses. So off we go in Norm's car for Waverly. Two days travel, both ways and our good friend Norm would drive all the way, round trip. He wouldn't let us share the driving because we may dent his car. When we arrived at our motel the evening before the auction, we had a nice dinner, showered up and a good night's sleep. Up early the next morning, and off to the sale yard after breakfast. When we arrived, the parking lot was already beginning to fill up with cars, trucks and Amish horse and buggies. We could hear the auction was well underway. Before we went in the barn, we went walking through the horse-drawn equipment and harnesses for sale outside. Inside the barn were the draft horses, mules, and some saddle horses that were being auctioned off. As I was walking towards the barn, I saw a goose neck horse trailer, 36 feet long with one full rear door and a side door ramp for loading horses. I looked around and then I found a red dray wagon loaded with chrome. It looked like a replica of the Budweiser hitch wagon. We kept walking around looking at everything, but my eyes kept going back to that trailer and wagon. We went into the barn to watch them sell a few teams, but my thoughts kept going back to that trailer and wagon.

Finally, I excused myself, went back outside to you know where. I saw a fella with a tape measure. I asked if I could use it for a few moments. I began to measure the wagon and the inside of the trailer. Come to find out the measurements of the wagon were exactly right to fit in that trailer that I had my eye on. Height, width and length. After talking it over with my brother, we made a deal for him to go back to Waverly in his truck and pick them up and deliver them to me in El Centro if I should happen to buy them. It came time to auction off the trailer, which the crowd started bidding. The folks bidding began to drop out of the bidding one or two at a time. And low and behold, I was the last man standing. I bought myself a great trailer for my Clydes. Then came the dray wagon, and again the same thing, the bidding started out. Again, when the dust settled, I was the last man standing. I now owned a 36 foot trailer and a beautiful red dray wagon. I wrote the auction company a check. Stan, Norm and I loaded the wagon in the back of the trailer, locked it up, and made arrangements to store it there until Stan could come back with his truck from Colorado and pick them up.

We had lunch at their restaurant at the sale yard, looked around some more and went out to the parking lot to leave. There was a guy sitting in a chair under a tent awning with some miniature buggies and wagons on display. I walked over to talk to him. I told him what I wanted. He told me if I would send him a picture of my wagon and my buggy, hooked up to my Clydes, he could match it in a pure leather harness and also match the wagon and buggy, and paint them any color I wanted. I told him I would be in touch with him because I wanted a model to sit on a shelf in my office at home. What a wonderful experience it was to go to Waverly for their nationally known auction. You should put Waverly on your bucket list.

On our return trip, we stopped at a truck stop just outside of North Platte, Nebraska for a cup of coffee. It was late at night. I noticed a young boy, about twelve years old, kept staring at me, and finally he came over to me and said to me, "I know who you are, sir. You are the guy that owns Tom and Jerry, the Clydesdale hitch that comes to Cheyenne every year to drive in our parades."

And I replied, "Yes, I am, son." and we small-talked a little bit. Stan and Norm are hollering at me, "Let's go, Jack." So, I shook the young man's hand and told him goodbye and hopefully, I'd see him again in Cheyenne. He got in his dad's truck and off they went to Cheyenne where he lived. It made me feel good to think there we were late at night, out on the plains of Nebraska and ran into someone that liked my horses and recognized me as their driver. From there to Montrose, I kept telling Norm to sell those black Percherons and get Clydesdales instead and become famous. My brother Stan and I wouldn't let up. We laughed all the way to Montrose.

In about two weeks, Stan delivered my trailer and wagon to me in El Centro. I went to work on it, painting it the same as our truck with western-styled signs painted on the sides. I installed a winch and a ramp so we could just hook the winch on the rear axle of the wagon, press the button and in it would go. I had two large white cabinets built and lined them with red carpet for Tom and Jerry's show harness and the big guys would load in the side ramp up front. They were tied in their stalls with plenty of hay in front of them and down the road we would go to the next parade. Now it sounds like my big brother was always at my beck and call, and he was, rest his soul. He made two different trips to Pierre, South Dakota to pick up two-year old Clydesdales that I bought and then he made a trip to Waverly to get our wagon and he also made several trips from Montrose delivering horses or taking horses back to Montrose. Yes, he was always there for me. Thanks Stan, you were a big part of my life.

Our Three-Seated Surrey

While we were in Amish country in Pennsylvania in the little town of Bird In Hand, we met a wagon maker, by the name of Ephraim King. I told Mr. King that I went to the auction they have there in that town and saw several buggies and wagons for sale, but not the type I was looking for. I told him I wanted a three seated surrey with a fringe on the top. I gave him my phone number and mailing address. He told me he goes to the auction every month and that he would keep an eye out for me for what I told him I wanted.

Mr. King called me in about two months. Now, being Amish, he had to go to town in his buggy to use a payphone to call me because the Amish do not have electricity, phones, or cars. No gas engines! Anyway, he told me there was one for sale. *Just what I wanted.* "How high should I bid?" he asked. I replied, "If you say it is exactly what I want and the wooden wheels are in perfect shape, buy it!!" He said, "I'll call you and let you know what happens."

In about two hours, I received a call and it was Mr. King. "Jack, I bought you a surrey." I replied, "Great, now how do I get it to California from Pennsylvania." He said to me, "I have a friend that will be leaving here soon with a truck load of mushrooms to Los Angeles, and he said he would be willing to swing by El Centro and bring your Surrey for $200." I told him, "Ship it!" and I thanked Mr. King for a job well done and mailed him a check.

Another two weeks went by and here rolled in our yard a big eighteen-wheeler. I opened the door and there sat the prettiest surrey you would ever want to see. We unloaded it and paid the man his money and he left. I just stood there looking at it. It had three black leather seats, a black leather top with a white fringe around it and yellow wheels. It couldn't have been more perfect than if I had it built. I offered to pay Mr. King for his time and he replied, "No, thanks.

Just glad to help you out." As I stood there and looked at my surrey, I looked up towards heaven and thanked the Lord for what he has done for me again. Mr. King could have cheated me on the auction price; the truck driver could have taken my surrey, 'cause I didn't know who he was, but all worked out for his glory.

The first thing I did the next morning, was harness up *Tom* and *Jerry* and head out for town, right down Main Street, stopping here and there, talking to people I knew. We would stop in front of the Cameo buffet of course where I have taken them many times over the years. Where our customers could see the Cameo Clydesdales, *Tom* and *Jerry*.

Different Jobs for Tom and Jerry

In 1985, we built an executive golf course in El Centro with John Ryerson, who had also built a 400-space R.V. and mobile home park around my golf course. I named it the Broken Spoke Golf Course, because we placed twenty old wagons on the course and almost all of them had a broken spoke. All the wagons were used in western movies, such as *Little House on the Prairie* and *How the West Was Won*. I used our team to do a lot of the work on the course such as floating the greens with them before planting the grass, leveling the fairways, and dragging huge weeds out. Here is a golf course built with real horse power. Of course, we also used heavy equipment.

We used them in many TV commercials for the Cameo buffet. In one TV commercial that we made for the Cameo, we copied a Bill Coors commercial. Down on Clark Road, they had cut down some huge eucalyptus trees up on the canal bank. They cut them up and sold them for firewood, but they left the huge stumps lying on top of the ground after they had dug them out. I supposed they were going to come back and haul them off, which they did much later; but before that happened I drove the boys over there. I threw a chain around a big one and pulled it home. The next day I went across the road to an empty all dirt field and dug a small hole to set that stump in. I went back to the barn and threw the work harness up on the boys. I hooked up to the chain around that stump and dragged it over to the hole and pulled it in.

We got the cameras all set up and ready to go. When they hollered, "Action," I asked for *Tom*. He was always my lead horse, but calling for *Tom* also cued *Jerry*, so they would hit their collars at the same time. That's where you get the power. If they don't go at the same time you get a "see-saw" effect and no power and then nothing moves. The cameras were rolling and the big boys pulled that stump out of the hole. Then I stopped my team, took off my hat and wiped the sweat off of my forehead with my forearm. I slapped my hat on my leg to knock the dust off and then the announcer said, "After a hard day's work clearing the land, a great meal at the Cameo Buffet just hits the spot."

Another commercial we made, we took the boys out in the desert with Robin Kirby and another young girl that knew how to ride horses. We used a slow motion camera this time. The girls had bridles and back pads only on the horses. We got them lined up and ready to go. They were to run their horses as fast as a Clydesdale could run, racing in and out of sage brush. When they hollered, "Action," they took off. We shot it over about three times to make sure we got it. When they played it back in slow motion it was beautiful. It was one of the first TV commercials we made for the Cameo. We also made a TV commercial for the Yamaha Motorcycle Company out in our sand dunes and up in the mountains. In the snow, we did a Christmas commercial for the Cameo.

How about accidents? Yes, we had a few. One was at the Cattle Call Rodeo arena. After I had circled the arena, I was heading for the gate straight out. I had them on a run and I dropped one line, no controls now. I thought to myself, *this is going to hurt, and this is going to hurt bad if they miss that gate or don't stop.* After they're out, we hit the gate straight on, and out the gate I hollered "WHOA!!!" Thank the Lord for voice commands. They understood and obeyed, and they came to a perfect stop. I jumped down off of the wagon. I picked up the line dragging on the ground and no one even noticed.

I've had a double tree break in a parade. We had one break in a rodeo arena, but survived. While breaking *Tonka* to drive, I hitched him to a doctor's carriage that we had, so down the lane to the road we went. All was going well. *Tonka* was so used to noise behind him from pulling steers, that noise was no problem. When I came home, I turned in the front gate and started down the lane to the barn on a trot. Now, *Barnie* the goat inside the arena, alongside of the lane charged at *Tonka* and ran his horns into the chain-linked fence. *Tonka* jumped sideways. We caught a right front wheel on a pasture post which stopped the buggy dead still, and that caused him to break the singletree. He left so fast and I had such a tight grip on the lines that he jerked me out of the buggy and buried my nose in the dirt. I plowed up about a ten foot furrow with my nose. All was well. *Tonka* ran to the barn to the hitching rail and stood there waiting for me to come take his harness off.

Another wreck I had happened with Marilyn's horse *Bucko*. I put a harness on him and hooked him up to the same buggy, and down the lane to the road for a mile or so then back home. Down the lane, no *Barnie* this time, we got to the barn and I did a "no-no". I just wasn't thinking. You always unhook your horse or team first, then put a halter strap around his neck and then take off the bridle, especially with a bronc like *Bucko*. After that, you put the halter on his head and buckle it. Here's what I did wrong with *Bucko*. He was still hooked to the buggy, and I reached up and took his bridle off. I didn't even have a halter in my hand. *Bucko* thought he was free to go in the pasture, I assume, so off he went with the buggy flying out behind him. As he rounded the hen house and windmill, it upset on the turn. The buggy broke loose from *Bucko*, and he kept running towards Taylor's house. He jumped all the pasture fences between our pasture and John's Corrals and finally stopped and just stood there eating from the haystack until I came to get him. I brought him home took off his harness and repaired a couple of straps that he broke. I put the buggy up on its wheels, made a repair or two, and put the buggy in the barn. I did my chores and walked down the lane. I sat down and thought about how bad that wreck could have been. Funny things do happen. Yes, there were a lot of them. I'll just give you two.

Every year we would take the Shetland hitch to the McCabe School Halloween Carnival Fundraiser for the PTA. After we got the Clydes, we retired the Shetland hitch from this job and used the Clydes. At one of the carnivals, we were going around the playground with about thirty kids and some parents on our hay rack. This one boy about six or seven and his dad were riding up front with me. One of my horses raised his tail and spread a little manure on the playground while he was walking along. This young man grabbed his nose and said "Ewwweee!" So I thought I would explain to him what happened.

I said, "Now wait a minute son. That is just a normal thing that animals do. You can use that for fertilizer. You can take it home and put it on your strawberries." The kid's dad said, "I don't know where you're from, but where we live we put cream and sugar on ours." Every Christmas Eve, I would take the team and hayrack over to the golf course and load it up with seniors, then drive around the park singing Christmas carols as we rode. Two senior ladies were riding up front to my left, with their legs hanging over the left side of the wagon. Now *Jerry* raised his tail and released some silent gas, but it was really a bad stinker. I noticed the two elderly ladies were fanning their noses and looking at each other and making a bad face, so I turned to the two ladies and said, "I am very sorry about that. I feel like I must apologize." They replied, "Oh! We thought it was the horse."

In Cheyenne after lunch, those teamsters that didn't want to go the rodeo would just sit around and quote poetry and tell stories. One of my all time favorite stories was about this old farmer who had a wife that just complained and nagged at him all the time. When he had enough he would go to the barn, throw a harness on his mule and go out on the field and plow. Well, there he was plowing and here came his wife screaming and complaining. She walked up behind the mule flailing her arms. Now the old mule had enough too, he kicked back and hit her directly in the head. After the funeral services, the preacher walked up to the husband and said, "Sam, I noticed when the ladies would come up to you and say something, you would always shake your head up and down. What were they saying to you?" He replied, "They were telling me what a fine friend she was and that they would miss her."

"But Sam", the preacher said, "When the men would come up to you and say something, I noticed you would shake your head sideways, meaning no. What were they saying to you?"

"They were wanting to know, if that mule was for sale."

Another one of my favorite stories was that this old cowboy had been riding fence all day in the heat and dust. Come late afternoon, he started back for the bunk house, crossed a shallow stream with his horse and stopped for a minute and looked at that creek. He told himself, "I think I'll take a bath right here, because the showers will be full when I get home." So he got off his horse and tied him up to a branch. He took off all his clothes and was splashing around in the water, splashing water under his arms and over his head and face. He happened to look up and see the boss's wife sitting on her horse looking down at him. He quickly looked around for something to cover up with, now there happened to be an old rusty washtub sitting in the creek. He reached down and grabbed it, covered himself in the front and said to her, "Ma'am, I know what you're thinking and I'm sorry." She said, "No, I know what you're thinking. You're thinking there's a bottom to that tub."

The only farming I did with my team was to disk up my pasture and John's also, and then plant our rye grass in October. Our pastures were alongside of the road, so you can imagine how many look-e-loos would stop along the road and watch *Tom* and *Jerry* going up and down those pastures. Lots of times, out would come the cameras. We were also the mascot for the Central High School football team. David Pritchard, FFA and metal shop teacher built the chariot that we would hook *Tom* and *Jerry* to, and they would dress me in a toga that would fly out behind me with a Roman Spartan helmet on my head. I would charge on to the field, with a sword raised high in victory at the half times. I would make a pass in front of the opponent's stand and then a fast run in front of the Central's stand with thousands of people cheering.

Loaded up and ready to go!

*Tom and Jerry during the groundbreaking for the Imperial County Historical Society's Pioneer Museum.
Photo courtesy of The Imperial Valley Press.*

Nicole, my granddaughter, getting ready to disk for me.

Robin, my daughter, on Jerry running the barrels at the Cattle Call Rodeo in Brawley, California.

*Me as Spartacus at the Spartan football game.
Photo courtesy of The Imperial Valley Press.*

Tom pulling my golf cart while I tee off for a quick round.

Tom pulling a float for the Christmas Parade—it was his first parade without his brother, Jerry. Two nurses, my mother, and her roommate are on the float.

Cheyenne Days

Summer vacation, 1981, away from all the cattle drives until October. We took our Clydes to Cheyenne for ten days of shoot-em-up cowboy days. My brother, Stan had told the parade wrangler, Paul Brugman, about my Clyde-hitch, and he said, "Oh man! Can you get him to come? We want him here for our Frontier Day Celebration." They were the last ten days of July every year, so we accepted the offer. We loaded up the fifth-wheel RV, the Clyde harness, and dray wagon and started for Cheyenne. Marilyn was pulling the fifth-wheel RV and I was pulling the Clydes. We left Montrose early one morning and east on Highway 50, up over Monarch Pass, which was the continental divide, 11,700 feet high. When we reached the top we stopped for a rest and discussed on how we were going to get down off of this mountain without crashing. I told Marilyn I would lead the way and for her to put her truck in low gear and I'll put my rig in low gear.

"Then I want you to stay close to me all the way down." I said. In the event her truck got away from her, she could bump up against my trailer and I could hold her back to keep her from going over the edge. I can't believe to this day how brave she was to do that. We both had CB radios, so we could talk to each other the whole time going down. I kept encouraging her on how well she was doing and we were going to make it down easy, and then go on to Denver where we had a little problem. We got separated on Denver's freeway system, but thanks to our CB radios, we were able to find each other again. However, I noticed a little panic in her voice until we were reunited on 25 North to Cheyenne, which was the start of 21 years in Old Cheyenne, and very exciting times were ahead.

There with new found friends, Cheyenne is where the pavement ends and the West begins. Stan and Viv were camp cooks for fifty wagon drivers and their wives along with special guests. Always well over 150 souls showed for lunch every day. We all got free RV hookups, one meal a day and tickets to 10 days of shoot-em up rodeos, chuckwagon races every evening, and the night shows with big name country singers. We had four parades during the ten days. Saturdays, Tuesdays, Thursdays, and Saturdays again five miles long.

We always saw a wreck of some kind. Once I was in camp, backing up my truck to the fence in my slot. I heard someone holler, "Look out!" When I looked up, there came a team and wagon around the corner full speed with two men hanging on, their eyes wide open. The wagon slid into my front bumper and threw the two men out over the hood of my truck, upset the wagon and down through the camp they went; totally destroying the wagon and finally stopping at a closed gate at the end of the alley. I checked out the two men and they were okay. These wrecks would happen because the parade wrangler always brought in some old broncos that had been out on pasture all winter, and only hooked up to a wagon once a year for *Frontier Days*. Wild and woolly, but it was always fun and exciting for the spectators as well as the drivers which had to be very experienced cowboys. Thank the Lord; we always had an outrider alongside of us in every parade to come to our rescue if we got in trouble. Then after the parade the best looking hitches always drove in the grand entry for the afternoon rodeo. Which of course, Tom and Jerry were always in the grand entry group. After several years and I had sold my team, Marilyn and I continued to go to *Frontier Days* and I would drive their old wild teams. Now Mondays, Wednesdays, and Fridays, we would hook up a well broke team to a hay rack, load on about thirty of us campers and head for Main St, where the Kiwanis club served a free breakfast to anybody and everybody, eight to ten thousand people each day. The lines were three blocks long and the grills cooking hot cakes were one block long. The hot cake cookers would flip the hotcakes over their heads and the boy scouts with trays would catch them, and then take them to the servers. The menu was hot cakes, ham, orange juice, coffee or milk and all at no charge to anyone. The lines moved fast, the way they had it set up. It was held in the parking lot downtown. They would bring in bales of hay for us to sit on facing a stage where there were guest singers and other entertainment for us. From 8:00AM to 11:00AM, after breakfast and a little shopping, we would load up the hay rack with our passengers and then back to the

So You Wanna Be a Cowboy?

rodeo campgrounds for a little rest, then lunch with Stan, Viv and Marilyn, then off we would go to the rodeo.

One rodeo we were about fifty feet from the world champion bull rider, Lane Frost, when he was bucked off his bull, then the bull turned back around while he was on the ground. The bull stabbed Lane with a horn in his back. Lane jumped up and took two steps towards us and dropped dead. A terrible thing to see, especially so close. Lane was such a nice, young man and a world champion. The next year, they had erected a huge statue of him on his bull, and it is at the museum on the rodeo grounds to this day.

We went back to our RV's for a rest and then back to the chuck wagon races in the evening. This event had four horses hooked to an old fashion chuck wagon. They would all line up; four chucks abreast, each with two outriders, holding their horses as well as the lead horses on the wagons. When the gun went off, the chucks had to go up and circle a barrel and then out on the track for a one mile run wide open. The outriders had to jump on their horses and catch up with their chuck wagon before reaching the finish line or lose points if they both weren't there at the finish, which would determine the winning chuck. Four races every evening, talk about wild!

Over the years, we have seen horses drop dead on the track after the race from a heart attack. We saw a lead horse stumble and go down with the other horses and the chuck wagon run up on top of them, and the driver go flying through the air, then they would haul the driver away in an ambulance of course. We saw one outrider get too close to his wagon and his horse stepped one foot to the end of the wagon that carried the cook stove and flipped him and his horse upside-down and cracked his head like an egg. So you want to be a cowboy? Outside of all this kind of entertainment, old Cheyenne has a lot of early history about the West. The state capitol building, museums, and shopping, all open to the public. So you see, it's not all bad, and there are good things to do also for the faint of heart. I would suggest that everyone should experience *Frontier Days* at least once in their lives. Put it on your bucket list.

Every year, we would grab a grandkid to take with us. We showed them country and landmarks that they probably would have never had the chance to see, such as the Grand Canyon, Four Corners Monument, interesting Old Durango, Colorado, and the historical old mining town of Silverton over the million dollar highway to Box

Canyon in Ouray, Colorado, then we'd visit with cousins in Montrose. We always stopped in Buena Vista and spend a couple of days with the Robb family, who took us white water rafting on the Arkansas River. One guy drowned the day before our first river ride and I didn't tell Grandma Marilyn until after our trip or I'm sure she wouldn't have gone or let the grandkids go. White water rafting, wow! Put it on your bucket list.

After we'd leave the Robb's, it was 150 miles to Denver and another 100 miles to Cheyenne. We always made the kids, before leaving El Centro, to memorize the states we will be visiting and their capitols before they could go with us and every once in a while, while driving along, I would ask them a state capitol and they would call out the state and then the other way around, and they would call out the capitol. They had them all memorized and would do very good on their test. Not bad for ten and twelve year old kids. We would go through ten or twelve states on our trip to Oregon. When we got to Cheyenne the year that my grandson, Bobby went with us, he wanted to be a cowboy and when the girls went with us, they wanted to meet a cowboy!

We left Cheyenne heading for Salt Lake City and the Great Salt Lake basin then on to Caldwell, Idaho. In Caldwell, there was a cheese factory that we could tour around and watch them make cheese. The kids were fascinated. We would buy a couple of pounds of curds for us to munch on while we travel. The kids had never heard of curds and were reluctant to bite into one, but after lots of coaxing and when they tasted 'em, they loved 'em. Then on to Corbett, Oregon on the scenic highway twenty miles upriver from Portland where we would spend the remaining part of the summer. The kids usually had to be back in school before we would get home to El Centro, so we would put them on a plane with tears running down their cheeks, and ours I might add, on a one way flight to San Diego, where their parents would pick them up and get them home in time for school.

So You Wanna Be a Cowboy?

*Pulling a hearse with **Tom** and **Jerry** in the Cheyenne Days Parade.*

*After **Tom** and **Jerry**, I used a different team for the next parade.*

Stan, my brother, getting ready to cook lunch for 150 people. Marilyn is helping.

Vivian (my sister in law) and Marilyn (right) serving lunch.

Ed and Connie Robb are hanging on in the back while the rafting guide is working the oars. Marilyn, Marsie (our granddaughter), and me getting ready for the rapids on the Arkansas River in Colorado.

Cheyenne Parade Wrecks

Over the years with driving teams in Cheyenne's *Frontier Days* parades, there were several accidents with horses and carriages that I heard about and saw with my own eyes. One happened two wagons in front of me and my hitch. We had just left the compound heading for downtown and the start of the parade. We were right under the airport approach to the runway and here comes a C-135 cargo plane in for a landing, right smack dab over the top of us on his final approach at about 200 feet altitude. It spooked all the horses in line that were in that immediate area, including the team I was driving. I got them turned to the right into a chain-linked fence that stopped them. The team up front turned left sharply and upset the buggy driven by a lady. It threw her out on the pavement. It peeled her hide a little, but it really upset her more than anything. Now, the team broke loose from the buggy and ran into the park wide open and straddled a tree. They were hooked together with a neck yoke and when that neck yoke hit that tree at the speed and power of the horses running, it just ripped that harness apart. The outriders went right into action, and caught the horses which were now going in separate directions. Thank the Lord, they were running in that large park with no people in it. *So you want to be a cowboy, huh?*

Another bad wreck we had in the parade one year happened when we were all standing in line in front of the state capitol building, where the parade starts. We were waiting for our turn to enter the starting area. I was driving *Tom* and *Jerry* hitched to the old hearse. The unit right in front of me was a single horse hitched to a two-wheel made sulky that was used in the old days. The mail man stood on the back like a chariot driver and delivered mail around the outskirts of town. The driver had let his horse get right up next to the buggy in front of him. The horse started rubbing his head on the buggy in front and off came his bridle, so off went the horse with the mail sulky flying out behind. It headed left from where we were in line and headed for a large grassy lawn around a government office building. There was a high school band all lined up waiting to fall in line in the parade. The driver was hanging on for dear life, his eyes about the size of silver dollars, when the sulky hit the curb, and it threw him up in the air and he landed on the lawn. The outriders went into action after the runaway, hollering at the band kids, "Get out of way!!" They started getting out of the way, quickly. The horse turned to his right, out on another street. His feet went out from under him and down he went and the outriders were right on top of him before he could get up on his feet. They got a halter rope on him and dallied it around the saddle horn of the outrider, while some of the other hands cleaned up the broken sulky parts. After the parade, when we got back to the rodeo grounds we found out that the old horse had hurt himself bad. The vet said he thought he had a broken hip when he fell on the concrete, so they had to put him down. Now the Cheyenne committee has a wagon repair building right on the grounds so they can repair the wagons whenever they get tore up.

    We were in another parade with a big team of gray Percherons about five or six wagons ahead of me that got spooked by a motorcycle and cut left, up over the hood of a car, wagon and all. The right hand horse ran his right leg down through the windshield and suffered an unbelievable cut from his shin bone up to his shoulder. The parade was over when this happened and we were well on our way back to the compound. After I got back, I unhitched my team, hung up their harness and put them in their pen. I checked on the grays, and the vet was already there and had the big boy full of pain meds. He was just standing there with his head down low while the vet was down on his knees sewing him up. No more parades this year for that big team. *So you think you want to be a cowboy, huh?*

Bill Coors and a New Harness

One summer after all the cattle, weighing in about 700 pounds plus had been taken into feed lots for the rest of their lives, the feed lots would put them on hot food for maximum weight gain and finish out their meat quality for good marbling and so on.

Marilyn and I would load up the RV and our horses, grab a grandkid or two and then start off for Montrose. This time we left early one morning in May. We arrived at Montrose just in time to go with Stan and his Cameo buffet crew to cater an annual banquet for the Coors Brewing Company and all his barley growers on the western slope of Colorado. Each year, the Coors Company would invite all the farmers and their families that grew his barley for the banquet in Delta, Colorado. Our Cameo always catered it for them. Bill Coors, the oldest son of the founder and CEO always came to speak, eat, and fellowship with the farmers and their families. Our Cameo crew were all wearing our Cameo hats that had the picture of our Clydesdales and their names. One of Mr. Coors's aides came over to Stan and me and asked us to please remove our hats with the Clydesdales on them. We asked her why. Then she replied the picture of Clydesdales on them might be offensive to Mr. Coors, because of his biggest competitor, Budweiser's Clydesdale hitch. We agreed, but after I met Bill Coors and had a lengthy conversation with him and of course, the CEO of that corporation, I felt in my mind that it would not have bothered him at all. He was not that small of a man to think like that, I'm sure. It was just the thoughts of some small "go for" coffee girl who was thinking for her employer and how he would feel. Bless her heart.

Now flash back to El Centro to explain the rest of the story at home. When I got there that fall, we had not had the hitch that long. I was always wanting to hook them up to anything just to watch them pull and drag something around for fun. I would harness them

So You Wanna Be a Cowboy?

up just to enjoy buckling all the buckles and snapping all the snaps and drive them from the ground walking behind them, around and around the hen house and windmill and then take off the harness again. I can honestly say that throwing that harness up on those giant backs, giving them voice commands like "Step over" or "Step back" or "Step up" all that to me was about 60 percent of the enjoyment of owning the hitch.

Now, I had seen one of Coors commercials on TV that showed a big team of Belgians that they had hooked to a huge tree trunk, sitting down in a hole. That teamster asked for his team and they hit their collars at the same time, and that big stump came out of that hole with ease. The commercial was after a hard day's work clearing the land. It was time to freshen up.

Well, I had a tree about 8 inches in diameter in the barn yard that had died during the summer. It so happened that day I had the boys in their heavy work harness. So I told myself, I had seen that team in the Coors commercial pull out that stump. I thought surely, these big boys can pull that eight inch tree out of the ground. I put my log chain around the tree trunk and I put it through a heavy iron ring hanging on the double tree. I got all set to see that tree come flying right out of the ground. I got the boys lined up in the direction I wanted to go, then I asked for them, "Alright, *Tom!*" and they leaned into their collars and the chain tightened. One more time I called Tom's name meaning more power. All of a sudden, that ring broke and it sounded like a 30-30 rifle going off. The double tree snapped up against their hind legs which startled them and we had a little foot race for about fifty feet before I could get them to stop. I looked the situation over, scratched my head and told myself, *"I know these big boys can get that tree out of the ground."* So now, I backed them to the chain around the tree again and got them lined up in the direction I wanted them to go, the iron ring was gone now, never did find it. I hooked them together and I led their chain directly to the double tree and then I asked for them. They moved up into their collars strained a little, then put the power into the effort and what happened next shocked me. All the years I have been harnessing horses and pulling, I never had this happen, but when 4000 pounds of muscle leans on something, then something is going to move or break, which it did. All four Hayme straps snapped and they had walked right through their harness and skinned it clear back to their flanks. Well the day was over now, no more pulling anything. I had harness to repair before we could do any pulling again.

Now back to Bill Coors in Colorado and our conversation that we were having. I told him "Bill, I kind of think you may owe me a harness for my team." He replied, "How's that Jack?" Then I launched into the story you just read about and what had happened to me. The reason, I told him, I had these troubles is because I saw his commercial with that team pulling the stump out of that hole. So, I tried it with my big team and tore up my harness and my tree was only eight inches in diameter, and it is still there in the ground.

He said, "Well Jack, did you dig around the tree and cut all the roots?" I answered, no. Then he told me they had a tractor dig that big hole and brought the stump in and just set it in the hole. All the team did was just pull the stump out and then he added, "Sorry Jack, you should have dug around the tree and cut the roots." We both had a good laugh. We finished the banquet and started loading for home in Montrose. I looked at Bill and he was still grinning. He cupped his hands around his mouth and said to me as I was walking away, "Sorry Jack, no harness for you." Lesson learned. I replied, "OK Bill, see you next year."

Celebrities

We would say of all the celebrities; city, county, state, and federal dignitaries, as well as professional athletes, Bob Hope stands out the most. Just think of all he has done for our country and servicemen and women in World War II, Korea and Vietnam. No doubt, Bob Hope would be the most famous celebrity we ever carried in our surrey with *Tom* and *Jerry*.

Marilyn and I were standing there, waiting for Bob to come. He drove up in his Chrysler, parked it alongside our surrey, got out, came over to Marilyn and I, stuck out his hand, and I stuck mine out in return to shake his hand. Then I introduced Marilyn and myself to him. We climbed up into our seats and began to talk as we waited for the program to start.

Bob began to talk to us about our horses, how long we had them and where we got them from and so on. Then he began to talk about his golf tournament that had just concluded, the Bob Hope Classic which was held in January every year. He was very gracious and friendly. Marilyn and I really enjoyed visiting with him. When he left us, he climbed down out of our surrey, turned and shook our hands and thanked us for the ride.

He said, "It was nice to have met you Marilyn and Jack, and especially thank you for taking part in our annual *Western Day Celebration* here in Palm Springs, certainly hope you can come back each year. We would certainly like to have you." One of his aides, Derrick Goodall was hanging around. Come to find out, Derrick was an official for the *Western Day Celebration* every year. So I got acquainted with Derrick over the years. I invited him and his wife, Margaret to come down to El Centro to play golf with Wes and me at my *Broken Spoke* golf course. He and his uncle, Charlie came. Margaret sent her regrets, but just could not make it this time.

We all played golf and then had lunch in the club house. I told Derrick that I had a picture of Bob receiving a plaque award and standing alongside of our Clydes. I told him I was going to have it enlarged so I could hang it on the wall in our Cameo restaurants. I would like to have it signed by Bob, but how can I get it past his employees that open his fan mail.

Derrick took out his pen and a notepad from his shirt pocket and said to me as he was writing an address on the pad, "Mail your picture to this address with a note reminding him about your Clydes and that you would like for him to autograph it for your restaurants."

Derrick told me that this address lands directly on the kitchen table and Bob opens all that mail personally. I mailed it to him at that address and about ten days later; here it came back to me in the same tube that I had mailed it to him earlier. We opened it, anxious to see if it had gotten to him because Derrick had told us that was his special address.

We unrolled the picture and there it said, "Jack and Marilyn, thanks for the memories. Bob Hope." How nice was that. The big picture that he actually signed is on the wall at the Cameo, and an 8 by 10 copy of that big picture is also on the wall at Camacho's today. We enjoyed all of our celebrities. Some were more interesting to us than others.

Norma Zimmer was as sweet as sugar. She was the Laurence Welk Champagne lady. Paul Burke and his wife, Lynn, were exceptional as well. We ran into both of them the other day at the Eisenhower Hospital. We were both getting blood tests and had a good visit remembering the *Western Day Celebration* with them in our carriage while sitting in the waiting room. Our greatest celebrities we ever had, and I'm not prejudice, were two of our grandbabies. We made a TV commercial for the Cameo starring Nicole and Katie Kirby. We set them up in our dining room and I would ask them yes and no questions about the Cameo, such as "Is the food good at the Cameo?" and they would shake their heads up and down and say "Yeth!"

"Does granddad take you to the Cameo a lot?", and they would shake their heads up and down and say, "Yeth!" and then my last question was, "Well why does granddad take you to the Cameo?" and they would say "Because he loves us!" They were so little and wiggly the whole time the cameras were running. They didn't talk that plain and that's why we would ask them only yes and no questions. Their last line was hard to understand. We had to film it over and over until we finally got one take that wasn't so bad. We put it on the air, and it turned out to be one of our best commercials for the Cameo that we ever made. We received so many phone calls asking what those little girls were saying at the end. People would come to eat and they would ask what those little girls were saying at the end. It turned out to be a very effective commercial. Even with Marilyn and I, people that knew us would see us, and the first thing they would ask, "What are your grandkids saying at the end?"

That year, when the *Tomato Festival* came around in Niland, I entered the girls in the parade. We hooked *Dusty*, our Shetland up to a sulky that I had with a big sign across the back that said, "The Cameo Kids." Nicole and Katie sat with Terri Kirby, Katie's mom. She sat in the middle and drove *Dusty*, with a little girl on each side of her. The people along the parade route really enjoyed the kids and would applaud and wave and the little girls would wave back. It was Terry's first time to drive a horse. She did very well and the entry right behind them was *Tom* and *Jerry*, the Cameo Clydes.

Claude Akins, the first celebrity at the Palm Springs Western Days.

So You Wanna Be a Cowboy?

Jimmy Rogers: Singer

Norma Zimmer, the "Champagne Lady" from The Lawrence Welk Show, riding in the wagon with me.

Paul Burke and Derrick Goodall (Bob Hope's butler) during the Palm Springs Western Days.

So You Wanna Be a Cowboy?

Bob Hope receiving his award for community service.

Chuck Connors

Weddings and Goodbyes

Over the years we had several weddings, one was in Colorado for a sheep herder and his bride. It was ten miles on a dirt trail, up in the high country, off of Highway 50. He wanted us to bring his bride and bridesmaids up to a meadow that they had picked out for a beautiful setting. We were using the three-seated surrey for the trip. We met the ladies about one mile from the meadow and loaded everyone in, eight people to be exact.

It was a pretty steep climb up the trail. *Tom* and *Jerry* had a good pull. All of the sudden, we hit the top of the hill and there in front of us was a hundred people or more standing in the setting that they had chosen. There was a barbed-wire fence close to where they were going to take their vows. Lined up behind that fence looking over, were twenty or more head of Heifer cows watching our every move.

When the actual ceremony started, the bride and groom were to say their own vows that they had written and memorized to say to each other. The bride went first and recited her beautiful words and then it was the grooms turn. He got started with a few words stuttering, trying to remember them. Then he stopped altogether and looked her in the eyes and said, "Honey, I forgot all I wanted to say to you. So all I can say is I promise you I will try my damnedest!" Big time laughter broke out from all, all except the preacher. When the wedding was over we had our refreshments and wished them all well.

The bride and groom left and went a little higher up on the mountain where they were to spend their honeymoon in his sheepherder tent, with his sheep all around them. A very unusual way to start your married life, herding sheep, but they were so happy.

We had one wedding at the Barbara Worth Country Club, Charles and Kathy Denton. Our job was to take them after the wedding, from the Barbara Worth Country Club to her folks' house, about two miles down Highway 8 to the research station. It was a wonderful day in our valley. It didn't take long, 'cause I had the boys on a fast trot. Their marriage had started out great and is still goin' on strong. We see them every Sunday at church.

We also did our daughter's wedding. After the wedding, our nephew John Wardrup drove them from the church to Jeans Station at the corner of Fourth St and Wake Ave. We were waiting for their arrival to change from the old antique Franklin car to the big red wagon with chrome shining in the sun. I put *Tom* and *Jerry* on a full trot. When we rounded the corner at the golf course, there was the reception party, applauding and taking pictures of Robbie with her brand new husband, Michael Martin. He was grinning from ear to ear. We made a lap around the park and back to the reception party. We unloaded the bride and groom. Bob Kirby secured the hitch until after the wedding. Lots of pictures were taken out on the number nine green, as well as at the clubhouse patio. Finally, they changed their clothes, said all their goodbyes, got in their car, and headed for the airport to catch their flight heading for the Fiji Islands down in the South Pacific, where they were to have their honeymoon. *Bon Voyage, kids, we love you!*

We only did one funeral and that was for Marilyn's dad, Burl Wardrup. Burl loved his horses as well as *Tom* and *Jerry*. After many years on the John Taylor main crew, he made his last move, as all of us will someday make, that final move. After the service at the church, the hearse took him to the front gate of the cemetery, and then we loaded grandpa into the rear of the wagon. We drove him through the cemetery to his final resting place alongside grandma, Thelma. I drove my team up alongside of his grave. The pallbearer slid his coffin to the rear of the wagon and carried him to his grave. It was a beautiful service with those big, beautiful Clydes, with their shining harness and white feathers. Granddad would have been so happy with his send off. I'll say this; that is exactly what I would like for myself when my time comes, but a big problem now is all our Clydes are gone. So, old granddad Burl did it for both of us. *Rest in peace granddad, we love you.*

So You Wanna Be a Cowboy?

Delivering Robin (my daughter) and Mike (her husband) to the Broken Spoke Golf Course for their wedding reception.

Taking Charles and Cathy Denton to their folk's home after their wedding.

Jack Kirby

Goodbye, Grandpa Burl. We love you.

Fair Time

During the *Date Festival* in Indio, I would take *Tom* and *Jerry* and our red dray wagon to do their parade. I would leave the team on the fairgrounds in a barn that they had provided for us. Fair-goers for ten days could walk through the barn and enjoy seeing them and pet them on their noses or neck. We would leave them for the full run of the fair. Each day we would hook them up and drive them all around the fairground, stopping for people to ask questions or stand alongside of them for pictures. After the *Date Festival* in Indio, comes the *California Mid-Winter Fair* for another full ten days, also to be on display and also to hook them up for the same thing: pictures, talking, and answering questions.

Besides all the fairs, parades, rodeos and special events that we would show them, we were also featured on the *Good Morning America* TV show and a special article in the American Sportsman Magazine. We also hauled the first load of lumber on to the property where they were to build the Pioneer Museum, with all the city and county dignitaries seated as we drove in with that load of lumber as a surprise to all who were gathered there for that celebration and dedication. Now, we have that beautiful Pioneer Museum. It is amazing, all the different cultures of our people that have lived here or are still living here in our Imperial Valley. If you are passing through our area, it is well worth your time to stop by and visit it. We also have a group of folks that sponsor the *Children's Fair* every year in Bucklin Park, named after George Bucklin, a Valley long time resident. They set up all kinds of booths for the kids and have a fishing derby in the pond that is centered in the park. We would take *Tom* and *Jerry* there and set up our portable corrals and let the folks pet them and take pictures. Thousands of folks would attend.

Speaking of our *California Mid-Winter Fair*, here's a little note about my precious wife, Marilyn. She started baking banana nut cakes. She calls it bread, but believe me they are delicious, moist cakes. Anyway, she started baking in late October as soon as we arrived home from Oregon. She bakes 130 cakes for Christmas and puts them in our freezer until Christmas Eve. Then she does all the wrapping of each cake. We stack them up in boxes load them in the back and front seat of our car or truck and then I start around 4:00AM Christmas morning delivering around town to kids' and friends' homes. While I'm delivering cakes, Marilyn is up at 4:30AM and starts preparing brunch for sixteen family members to have at 10:00AM. I take the cakes up to the front doors and lay them on the steps while I ring my sleigh bells up to the door and back to the car with some big *Ho-Ho-Ho's!* and *Merry Christmas!* Some of Santa's accounts would leave me a plate of cookies or homemade candy on a chair in front of the door, knowing that old Santa would be there. I never missed it in 37 years. It's fun when the little kids sometimes hear the bells, throw open their curtains and catch me running to the car. I can hear them hollering, "Momma, momma! He's here!"

We have kept records for fun on the ingredients that she has used over the 37 years. Sorry, I won't give you her recipe because she is the Blue Ribbon Champion at our *California Mid-Winter Fair*. After my urging her to enter, she finally did and won her Blue Ribbon, First place. Listed below is the volume she has used over the 37 years to make 3,355 cakes. She has used 6,700 eggs; 13,400 bananas; 840 pounds of margarine; 5,025 pounds of flour; 5025 pounds of sugar; 1,675 pounds of pecans, and all this cost about $6,425.00. *Lots of fun.* I have asked her to slow down now after all these years, but the Blue Ribbon gave her new steam.

Another job for Jack was when I went into the fair office to get Marilyn's application for entry. I just asked the lady in the office, if they had any openings for people on the gate. She said, "Yes, we do." She handled me an application and I filled it out. I handed it back, thanked her, and left. They called me the next week and told me to come in for orientation and I did. My shifts were four hours a day for four days, and two days for eight hours, and off the rest of the week. The job was to sit on a stool and stamp the back hands of people leaving that wanted to return. *So seniors, just ask. There's a job waiting for you.*

So You Wanna Be a Cowboy?

An added note one year a police officer saw me running from house to house and stopped me. He wrote me a ticket for an out of date license tag on my Lincoln and said he had to tow my car because it was out of date. I told him I am Santa, look at all these packages that I have to deliver. He said, "Sorry Santa, I still have to give you a ticket, but I won't tow your car. "Report to court on Monday," the officer said. That's probably the first traffic ticket that even the real Santa ever got. I still have the ticket, and I have it framed.

A Tribute to My Friend

The sound of massive hoofs hitting the pavement, as two tons of black Clydesdale high stepping down one of the streets of El Centro, pulling a hay wagon loaded with kids. A surrey with a fringe on top and a happy bride and groom in the back seat enjoying the ride from the church to the reception, or a wagon full of kids at a *Western Day* celebration at some of our churches throughout the Valley towns. Load after load of tourists from motels and conventions in Montrose, Colorado during the summertime or transporting a dignitary in parades, or into an arena for introductions and events all over the southwest. Exciting football fans when charging onto the field, hitched to a chariot at half-time, and at his last parade, watching faces light up with thrills and admiration as *Tom* and *Jerry*, the Cameo Clydesdales brought Santa to town in this year's Christmas parade. Struggling to keep up with *Tom*, he wouldn't quit as I talked to him all the way through.

Two tons of matched Clydesdales, brothers by birth, a team by destiny, they traveled throughout southern California, Arizona, Nevada, Wyoming, Nebraska and Colorado, proudly bearing the banner of the Cameo Buffet. Often the name of the restaurants they represented were forgotten, but rarely, if ever, did their fans forget *Tom* and *Jerry*. It was an experience of a lifetime to sit behind that gentle, giant team with their great power and gentleness, and watch them respond so carefully to my voice commands and tugs on the lines as they would move heavy loads for me, one being over four tons of dead weight.

I stood in the pasture today, just a few feet from *Jerry*, just looking at him and remembering all the joy he had given me over the years. Then he moved what was once a massive body, now reduced to a frail one, and placed his forehead against my chest and held it there.

Somehow I knew he was telling me his time had come. When he was laying in the pasture resting, his brother *Tom*, never left his side. Sadly, I convey to his friends and admirers that his traveling days with his brother, *Tom*, as a team are over. *Jerry* died quietly of a liver ailment in El Centro, CA at the age of twenty years. *Jerry* was truly a beautiful, gentle giant in every respect and though he is gone. He will be remembered by people who loved and admired him, and especially by Marilyn and me. I thank God for giving me this great opportunity to share one of his wonderful creations with so many people. *Goodbye,* Jerry. *A job well done.* I received a letter today of condolences from the University of California Davis who had been working on his liver disease.

It was one of our perfect, beautiful, cool mornings. I walked down to the barn, put a halter on Jerry and took him out of the barn and just sat on a bench. We were looking at each other. You talk about tears, as I looked at that gentle giant that had given me, my family, and literally hundreds of thousands of people so much joy. I remembered when I would drive the boys down Main St to the Cameo, I would look for people walking on the sidewalk with a frown on their face, maybe they just came out of an attorney's office (which would explain the frown), and then all of the sudden out of the corner of their eye, they would see *Tom* and *Jerry*. They would always stop and their countenance would completely change and that frown would change into a big smile, and a wave would usually follow.

I was thinking of all these things that had happened over the years. My pastor stopped by that morning to offer me some comfort. Well, here came Dr. Thompson down the lane and I knew our time had run out. I got up off of the bench and walked *Jerry* over to a clearing in the barn yard so the tractor could pick him up. I put a chain around his hips and flanks and a chain around his waist, close to his front legs. The vet stepped up, found an artery in his neck and injected the needle while I was holding his halter. He said, "Jack you've got about ten seconds." I gave him a cube of sugar and patted him on his neck. Just then *Tom* was looking out the half door of the barn and nickered. *Jerry* took the sugar cube, turned his head, looked over at his brother, *Tom*, and then fell to the ground. The vet checked his eyes and determined that he was dead. We hooked the chain to the tractor and Elden Hunt, my good friend, who was driving the tractor, took him over to the hole that he had dug for me earlier. I placed a plastic bag over his head so the dirt wouldn't get in his eyes. Then Elden laid him gently in his grave, pulled out the chains, and pushed in the dirt. That was the close of the happiest era in our lives. For two weeks, *Tom* walked from one end of the pasture to the other, nickering for his brother, *Jerry*.

This was taken a few days before Jerry died. His brother, Tom, wouldn't leave his side.

So You Wanna Be a Cowboy?

After Jerry died, Tom continued to look for his brother.

Two New Tom and Jerry's

After we had to put Jerry down, I was looking for a replacement for him. While at the auction in Waterloo, Iowa, I was told about the ex-lieutenant governor of South Dakota that owned a buffalo ranch just a few miles from Pierre, South Dakota. If you saw the movie *Dances with Wolves*, that ranch is where they filmed it, on the Triple U ranch owned by Mr. Roy Houck. He had 3500 head of buffalo, 300 head of horse, and a 100 head of black Clydesdale horses. Of course you saw the buffalo and saddle horses in the movie, but they kept the Clydes out of the filming.

The adobe hut that Kevin Costner took over in the movie was still there. Roy's daughter, Kay asked if we would like to see it, and we all said sure. We piled in her Jeep and took off over the rolling hills of South Dakota and came up on it, and the little lake was still there. I was fooled by the structure of the building. It wasn't adobe blocks as it seemed to be in the movie, but was made of plastic blocks that looked exactly like adobe. Then Kay took us to see buffalo and horses, and after that, on to see a herd of black Clydesdales on her 50,000 acre ranch. We drove right up, next to the Clydes. I was looking them all over, looking for a certain color and finally spotted a two-year old colt that was marked. It was exactly what I wanted, with excellent white feathers on his legs. I showed her that was the one I wanted, the one that had a special mark on his forehead. Kay said, "Okay, he's yours. I'll remember that mark, and when you come to get him, I'll load him up for you."

Now, he had never been in a trailer before, so when my brother Stan went to pick him up for me, they had to use the tractor to push him in. After he was in, they gave him a generous serving of hay. Stan then started on his way home with my cargo, and he rode just fine. They are very docile animals, so when they arrived in Montrose they unloaded him, and he lay down and rolled over and over on his back.

The next morning when they were going on the next leg home to El Centro, he walked right in on the trailer. After he arrived in el Centro, I let him run in the pasture and let him get acquainted with *Tom*. After a week, I thought; *well let's see what we got here.* So, I harnessed Tom. I started slow and put the collar and harness on the colt. No problem so far. He didn't fight me like saddle horses have done when breaking them. I hooked *Tom* up first on the right side, and then I pushed and shoved the new *Jerry* in place. I hooked him up to the doubletrees on his side and climbed up on the seat. I told Marilyn, "Stand back honey, let's see what we've got." I asked for *Tom* by always calling out his name and *Tom* hit the collar and started to move forward. Young *Jerry* just stood there, not knowing what to do. When he felt pressure on the britchon straps around his rear end, *Tom* was able to drag him for a few steps, and then he went right along with *Tom*. I knew that if he acted up, old *Tom* would reach over and bite him on his neck. In horse language, that meant, "Straighten up young man and follow me. This is your job now."

We went down the lane and out to the road and turned right. Another new move, turning. So, Tom had to pull him over. So while going down the road, I would make a lot of S-turns, right and left, so he would feel the pull on his lines and get used to the signals. After going so far, I turned around to start home. After the turn was completed, he went straight in the air.

My first thought was, *well here we go. Watch out friends, looks like we are about to experience some pain,* but good old *Tom* just held him steady. I stopped them and let them stand still for a couple of minutes. Then I asked for *Tom* and we headed on home. Four thousand pounds of muscle were pulling that wagon so I was expecting a runaway, but that's why they call them gentle giants. A few more hitches and they were ready for a parade. *Tom* was getting real old and I wanted to replace him so we could have a young *Tom* and *Jerry* and then send old *Tom* out to pasture with "a job well done." So, I sent Stan back to Pierre, South Dakota to pick up another matching colt. I broke him alongside of *Tom,* and then hooked him up with the new *Jerry*. There we were with the new hitch representing the Cameo Buffet and the Valley Independent Bank. I finally sold the team to Mel and Margo Lamoreaux and they continue the service with the new bank, Rabobank. Mel bought a new show harness, and so he gave the old one back to me. *Tom's* harness is on display at our Pioneer Museum on Aten Road and Highway 111.

I used old *Tom* to pull my golf cart or drag an old dead tree off the golf course or I would hook him up to an old wagon I had and let the little granddaughters drive him around or ride on his back while I was driving him around the park. In the end, it was a wonderful era in Marilyn's and my life.

The new Tom and Jerry.

Old Tom showing that he can still run with the young boys.

The new Tom and Jerry together for the first time with old Tom.

New Jerry and our granddaughter, Taryn, in the pasture at Kirbyland U.S.A.

Kirbyland U.S.A.

In 1971, we bought our acreage from John Taylor and built our country home and called it *Kirbyland, USA*. It was 4,000 square feet, had four bedrooms and four bathrooms; 18 rooms including a wonderful office for me. We wanted a big house to finish up our family before Marilyn and I downsized. We got 'em all married including Paul and Terry who were married in the house.

I hired three carpenters and between us, we built the barn and the house. It took me one year to build it. We used all redwood. The barn had a hayloft with two stalls inside, and two roof covered pens outside the barn. There were four outside pens, a wash-rack for our horses, a fenced-in pasture and arena. I used two-inch water pipe, all painted white. We built a pig pen for Robin's FFA pigs that would show at the fair. She also had two Nubian goats for her pets, she named them *Arnie* and *Barnie*. She got them when they were babies, so they grew up thinking she was their mom. She bottled-fed them until they could eat hay and grass.

I always kept three roping steers and a couple calf-roping-sized calves. I built a great hen house with a laying nest on a slope, so when the hens laid their eggs, they would roll down into a catch screen outside the hen house. We could just walk along the catch screen and gather the eggs without going inside. Of course, the kids all wanted a swimming pool with a sun deck and a bridge. The bridge went from the sun deck across the pool to a waterfall at the corner of the house. *Lots of fun, you can imagine.*

We started with one Shetland pony, *Dusty*, for the boys. I broke him to drive to a four wheel, two-seated cart. He was a purebred, registered Shetland while we were still living in town. We kept him in a pen in the corner of our lot by our pool. The neighbors never complained about him for two reasons: Paul would give all the kids rides on the wagon and they would all swim in our pool, so no complaints. He was so small, 30 inches tall and very gentle for the kids on the block. We kept his pen clean at all times. When we sold our home in town and built *Kirbyland*, of course Dusty moved to the farm. *Tonka* and *Tonka Jr.* moved their also. We began to buy Shetlands to match *Dusty*. I wanted at least a six-horse hitch, so the first addition was *Samantha*, and then came *Tyrone*, *Cyndi*, and *Sugar* and *Spice*. We had matching harnesses for all six. One day I said to Marilyn, "Let's harness 'em up and see what we have." So we hooked them all up to a wagon I have. *Sugar* and *Spice* were the wheelers, *Tyrone* and *Cyndi* were the body team, and *Dusty* and *Samantha* were my leaders.

We did this in the arena, so if we had a runaway, they couldn't go too far, because it was fenced on all four sides. I climbed on the wagon, took the lines in my hand and told Marilyn, who was holding them steady, "Turn' em loose and jump back." *Samantha* and *Dusty* were well broke and I knew they could and would do their best to hold them all steady. To our surprise, when I asked for my lead team by calling *Dusty* by name, they started to move forward. At that point, I applied pressure on the other four ponies and they all started moving together following *Dusty* and *Samantha*. Now, I had driven each of the others a few times, by just walking behind them so they had some idea as to what was going on. *Wow! We've got a six-up hitch!*

After more driving them up and down the road all hitched together, they were ready for their first parade, which was the coming up Christmas parade with Santa Claus and wrapped Christmas gifts all over the wagon. Santa would be up on the seat with me. Many other parades like Palm Springs' *Western Days*, the *Silver Spur Rodeo Parade* in Yuma, and others we would advertise our Cameo Buffet. My Uncle Orin Smith called me one day from Colorado. He had found a miniature horse lost way up in the mountains of Colorado and wanted to know if I wanted him, before the bears and mountain lions got to him.

"Sure.", I replied. So off we went to Montrose to get him. I told everybody that I was going to Colorado to pick up a wild stallion, so immediately I named him *Thunder*. When I got there, I saw a shaggy, palomino-colored, emaciated pony needing grain, vitamins, hay, and just good care and lots of love. After a few months, he developed into a beautiful, little stud, 26 inches tall. We bred our mares to him which is another story, but the mares would always throw great babies. After they were weaned we would have a 'name that baby horse contest' at the Cameo and win a bicycle. I built a corral in front of the Cameo in the street and we would put momma with her baby on display in the corral. People just packed around to see that baby. Then hopefully, go in the Cameo for lunch and get an entrance form. We would have a drawing and the winning draw would get the new shiny bike. A very successful advertising idea and at home we kept *Thunder* busy making babies. We also had a Banti rooster named *Dynamite*, who was just as busy as *Thunder* making baby chicks. Those two guys were well named.

Kirbyland U.S.A.

T.V. stars, "The Cameo Kids," on Easter Sunday before church.

Me and Thunder

Britt, our foreign exchange student from Sweden, with Thunder's first colt.

Our 6 matching pony hitch bringing Santa to town. Dusty is the right lead.

Marilyn's Duck Named Dugan

(Written by Marilyn Kirby)

This story begins in 1975 when a long time friend of ours in San Diego found a Mallard duck that had been mauled by a dog and could not fly. They lived in the inner city of San Diego and could not keep it, so they brought him to me in El Centro because we lived in the country and had ducks and chickens. Somehow he got the name of *Dugan Duck*. It stuck with him for the two years we had him.

My husband built a ramp for him to walk up to the horse watering tank so he could swim. I would go out to the barn and doctor him every day with Carona Salve, which we used on the horses for cuts, so he began to heal slowly.

Dugan bonded with me so closely that he wanted to be with me all the time. One day, while I was working out on the patio, I happened to look out towards the barn and there came *Dugan* on his first flight since his injury. He landed in our pool and after a good swim; he climbed out and followed me all around the patio while I did my work. I would talk to him constantly and he would quack back at me as if he understood everything I was saying to him.

It wasn't long until he took up with the kids and when they would go swimming, he would go in the pool and swim with them. When they would go under the water to hide from him, he would dive down under the water and grab them by the hair until they would surface. I don't know if he was concerned about them being under water or if he was just playing.

After a few weeks of him growing stronger, he began taking off on longer flights, about half-mile circles around the place. I began to worry he would eventually fly away, so I would go out in the pasture where he could see me and when he would fly by I would holler at him, "*Dugan*, you come down here right now!", and on his next pass he would crash land at my feet. I would scold him and he would just quack and waddle behind me back to the patio.

It wasn't long while on some of his distant flights, he discovered our neighbor's swimming pool, and he started landing in it for a swim. One day, my neighbor, John Taylor, called us and said, "Jack, you have to do something with this duck, he is in my pool every day." So my husband told him, "Just pick him up and throw him up in the air and he'll fly home." John replied, "I've thrown him up so many times, my arms feel like they're going to fall right off!" I knew then that we would have to do something with *Dugan*.

We were on our way, in our RV, to Colorado for our summer vacation. Jack put a large wire cage in the back of the pickup and off we went for Montrose, Colorado with *Dugan* in the back. While there, we found a small lake with Mallards on it. I let *Dugan* loose on the edge of the water and when I did, all the other ducks came running after him, attacking. He came to me as fast as he could waddle.

There were some toolies and willows on another small lake across the road, so we took him through the growth and released him again where he could not see us while we took off running for our truck. When we got to the truck, guess who was on our heels? *Dugan Duck!* We decided he would not stay there, so we took him back to the RV. A few days later we took off for Oregon, of course with *Dugan*.

We arrived in Corbett, Oregon at my cousin's house where he had ducks and geese, and we thought, "*My, this is just the place.*" We put him in the pen with my cousin's ducks and geese and he just waddled back and forth quacking constantly. I couldn't stand to see him so unhappy, so when we left to go home to El Centro, we loaded *Dugan* back in his cage in the back of our pickup and started home. When we would stop at RV parks for the night, I would take him out for a walk like the other folks would take their dogs.

Upon arriving home, my brother brought by a female Mallard and you know what happened next? Tada! Eight baby Mallards running about, and so now we had ten problems instead of one!

We were going to Newport to visit my other brother, Larry. We had talked to Larry and told him about our duck problem and he told us to bring up *Dugan* and his family and release them on his golf course where they had hundreds of ducks on their lakes, and so we did. It was a successful release. As we watched them swim off, it was very emotional for me, but I knew it had to be done.

One year later, we were back in Newport for a weekend at my brother's house, so I thought we could go down to the golf course lakes and see if we could spot *Dugan*. He would be easy to find because he had a top notch on the back of his head that hadn't healed right because of his injury, so the feathers on his head stuck straight up.

There were hundreds of ducks on the pond and I thought it would be impossible to find him, but I began to call him anyway, hoping to get a glimpse of my *Dugan Duck*.

All of the sudden, out of the pack came a duck with a top notch on the back of his head. He swam to shore and waddled his way to me, so I knelt down and he came up and nibbled on my fingers as if to say, *Hi Marilyn, I'm okay. My family is raised and I want to thank you for bringing me to this wonderful place.* He turned and went back to the water and swam across the lake to the other ducks. It was amazing how he remembered me after a whole year had gone by. As we walked away, I turned for one more glimpse of my feathered friend. I knew this would be the last time I would ever see *Dugan*. I have often thought of him and have been so thankful to God for giving me the chance to help my little troubled friend and for giving him a second chance at life.

Molly and Friends

Paulie, our number one son, gave his little sister, Robbie a black baby pig for Christmas one year to raise and make some money for her efforts, so she could have a little cash to spend. She took good care of him, got him up to 225 plus pounds, just the right size to butcher for some good festivities. The month of June came around. It was a typical hot summer day. I was out at the barn and I noticed the pig breathing hard with his mouth open and obviously he was too hot. So I grabbed the hose and coiled it up laying there by the horse tank and pulled it over to his pen and began to spray him down with cold water all over his body. He began to squeal real loud and the more he squealed the more I laughed and said to myself, "Look how much he likes that. Just listen to him." He finally fell and just laid there. I turned the water off and went back to his pen and found he was dead, apparently shocked from the cold water. I loaded him in my horse trailer. When Robin came home I told her what had happened and Robin said, "Nah-uh!" I said, "Yes." and she said again "Nah-uh!" I said "Yes, he did, Robin. Go look in the horse trailer."

So out the door she flew, climbed up on the trailer and looked in. Sure enough, her pig was dead and her dreams of being rich were gone. I told Kenny Holmes, my FFA teacher back in the '40's in high school, the next Sunday morning at church, what I had done to Robbie's pig. He said, "Oh no! Too much shock for that sized pig." He said pigs cool themselves in mud and water by lying on their bellies, not all over their backs. Lesson learned! I told my garbage man that picks up garbage at the Cameo, what I did. So he sold me another baby pig. Robbie raised this one to butcher size.

While she was at school, a couple of fellers came by wanting to buy her pig. I sold him for a hundred dollars. When Robbie got home from school, she was delighted, finally she was rich. She wanted another pig, so I got her another baby pig from my friend. She was red with a stripe around her middle. Now, that baby pig was raised in the house the first three months of her life. Robbie named her Mollie. We would take her out on the front yard to do her business. When she was through, she would scratch on the door like our dog and then she would come in running. Robbie kept her bathed and covered with perfume all the time that Mollie was in the house, a lot of fun to be around. I taught her to sit down when I would tell her to. Sugar cubes of course, she really loved them. Occasionally, I would take her to town with me, just for fun. I even let her follow me in the bank one time and to the Cameo several times. We would walk through the front door, walking right through the booth and tables with people eating. I heard one lady say to her friend, "was that a dog I just saw or a pig?"

Robin would take a nap in the big bean bag we had in the front room and Mollie would cuddle up in her arms and they both would go to sleep. When Marilyn would be working in the kitchen fixing dinner or something, Mollie would go through the lower cabinets and push the pots and pans out on the kitchen floor, pushing them around and around, grunting as she goes. Of course, everything had to be washed and put back. I came home one afternoon and found Robbie and that forty pound pig asleep up on the couch. Right then and there I said, "Robin, it's time Mollie moves to the barn." With a sorrow face, Robbie said, "OK dad." Reluctantly, she took Mollie down the lane to the barn, where she could enjoy the sunshine and then go in the barn also.

The first evening we came home from dinner at the Cameo, our headlights from the car shot back towards the barn. When she saw those lights, she began squealing at the top of her lungs and climbing with her front legs up on the chain-linked fence in her pen. It was to be her first night alone from Robin and outside for her first time. Every evening when we were at the barn doing our chores, feeding all the animals then start down the lane to the house, she would start her squealing, jumping up on her fence, wanting to go to the house. We all felt sorry for her, but that's the way it has to be when you're a pig.

One day when she was full grown and used to living outside, our neighbor wanted to buy her for breeding, so Robin sold her if he would promise not to eat her and just raise babies. He agreed, so Robin collected her money and was now richer than ever. She still had Arnie and Barnie that she had raised on the bottle since they were babies. Those two goats loved her and she loved them. It was a great experience for the whole family.

Molly learning how to sit.

The P.G.A. Tour

In 1991, we had sold the golf course and of course, John retired; no more cattle. My brother, Stan and his wife, Viv were working on the PGA Tour for two brothers, John and Mike Mastroianni. These two young men had started a company called Hole-N-One Sports Catering, Inc. They contract with the golf courses where tournaments are to be held. They cater to corporate boxes, hospitality tents and refreshment tents out on the course. I had finally retired from everything including cowboy life after 24 years at that. We had sold our restaurants, the golf course, and the farm. So, Marilyn and I were now foot loose and fancy-free. The Bob Hope Classic was going on so Stan asked us to come up to Palm Springs and enjoy the classic tournament. Marilyn and I went up, got our passes that his boss had given him for us and we spent some time with him watching what he and Viv were doing on the job. Marilyn and I looked at each other and then I said to her, "Honey, I think I would like to do this, how about you?" She replied immediately, "Why not?" I asked Stan, "Do you think they would hire us." He said, "I don't know go and ask them. That's them over there standing by that big tent." So, we moseyed on over there, and I introduced Marilyn and myself to each of them and asked them if they needed or could use another senior couple to travel with them on the Tour. Their reply was, "Sure, can you start today?" I said, "Sure, why not?"

Mike told us where to go with Stan and Viv to get our training on what to do and how to take cash fast and furious as well as how they wanted things done. That was the start of twenty years of another page in our lives. We saw those two young men and their family; their kids grow up through grade and high school, and even college. Now, some of them are married. John's daughter, Allison has made John and Debbie grandparents twice now. One of Mike's sons is married also and has just presented him and Terry with a granddaughter. He and Terry have three sons. In the summertime, they would travel with their parents and hang out at our concession stands, then go over to one of the other stands for a while. We had so much fun with those kids. Over the years they have been so good to all of us working for them. There were about ten senior citizen couples with RVs that would follow them from tournament to tournament. We would fellowship with each other at the R.V. park in the evenings. The bosses would take us all to Laughlin, Nevada for a three-day Christmas party, hotel, and meals, and even some money to play the slots. There were cruises from Long Beach to Mexico and they supplied us with company shirts and hats, meals and beverages, and also paid for our RV spaces when traveling. We were able to see the finest golf courses in the world and actually play on some of them on the Mondays after the Sunday tournaments at no charge. We worked tournaments in Canada, Washington, Oregon, California, Nevada, Arizona, Colorado, Kansas, Louisiana, Texas, Illinois, Florida, and the Congressional Country Club in DC. All three tours PGA, Seniors, as well as the Ladies PGA.

Over the years we got acquainted with Arnold Palmer and his wife, Kit. He gave me a copy of the putter he used to win his first 40 tournaments: Fuzzy Zeller, David Stockton, Dave Jr., Billy Mayfair, Bo Van Pelt and many others. It was a good run, but at 81 we cut back to only four tournaments all in California, starting with the Bob Hope Classic at Palm Springs in January. We also did The L.A. Open at the Riviera in February, the Reno/Tahoe open at Reno during July and on our way home to El Centro from our home in Corbett, the San Jose Tournament in the middle of October. The boys would always let Marilyn and I have time off to do the other things that you have been reading about in our book. They were two wonderful families to work for.

We don't know what is next in our lives except to enjoy each other, our three kids, nine grandkids, and six great grandkids, play a little golf, and go to our church every Sunday to study for our finals. It's the church that I have attended and sat in the same pew for 74 years with my parents and siblings all lined up along side of each other. Marilyn and I were married there 58 years ago, and since then, we have been going there together with our kids and grandkids. *Now, you understand, hey where's that bucket.*

So You Wanna Be a Cowboy?

As you know we always took a grandkid with us when they were small on our travels and their parents would let them go. We haven't had any kids travel with us for two years now, but my nephew, Steve called and said his son, Cole was sixteen years old, and has never seen the Pacific Ocean. He wondered if we could take him to Oregon with us from El Centro to San Diego, up the 101. So, he will be traveling with us this summer and Aunt Marilyn and I are already planning on some wonderful things to show him up the coast and in Oregon where we live.

Our bosses, Mike and John Mastroianni, on the P.G.A. Tour. They own Hole-N-One Sports Catering.

Dave Stockton and me at a P.G.A. tournament in Canada.

Silverado Country Club - Napa Valley, California - Arnold Palmer and I having lunch, during which he told me that this was his last tournament on the Champions Tour.

Hudson and Waterloo, Iowa

Stan, Viv, Marilyn and I left Coffeeville, Kansas and went to Kansas City. We had dinner at the Spaghetti Factory with our dear friend, Gwen McGuire, who was living in Kansas City, then back to our R.V.'s for the night. Our granddad, Tom Kirby's, family secret came out after we buried our dad. Our cousins that came down for his funeral, got Stan and I together away from mom and asked us if we knew the family secret about granddad, Tom Kirby. We both replied *no*. So they said, now that our dad was gone, "we feel that we can tell you now, that old granddad robbed a bank in Oakland, Iowa in 1897. After the robbery, he got on his horse and started out of town full speed. When they shot him off his horse, he was sentenced to just one year in Leavenworth Federal Pen. He only got one year because they got all the money back."

So Stan and I went out on the patio where mom was going through family pictures after dad's funeral. We asked her, "Mom what's this about granddad working in banks?"

She said, "What!!"

Then I said, "Mom we know he robbed a bank and went to prison."

My mom through her hands in the air. "Oh no!! Who told you boys that?"

"Birtie and Bob just told us."

"Oh! My goodness that has been a family secret for over 75 years."

Mom told us boys; don't tell your children or your grandchildren. Don't tell anyone ever, but Stan and I thought it was a great conversational piece, but we could understand how mom felt about it.

Now granddad came to California in 1939 to spend a two-week visit and stayed 14 years. Despite what he did, we all loved the old guy. Mom did his washing, ironing and cooked all his meals for him. I remember he had a bad sore or a wound below his knee that would never heal. Mom very patiently would clean it, put medicine on it and bandaged it whenever it needed it. I remember asking mom what happened to granddad's leg.

She would always say, "Well we don't really know and he can't remember." So we just take care of it for him. After granddad died, we were told by family members it was where he got shot in the bank robbery and got infection in the bone and it would never heal. While we were in Kansas, we drove out to the penitentiary just to see it. I bought a postcard picture of the prison. I circled a window with my pen and wrote on the card.

When I got home to El Centro, I told mom the window circled was granddad's cell. Mom was furious about the card. Now, she said, everybody in the post office and probably all over town knows about your granddad robbing the bank. After the visit to the penitentiary, we drove over to the University of Kansas to see the only survivor of the battle of the Little Big Horn and Custer's last stand. When visiting Custer's monument in Montana we were told about Lt. Keogh's horse, *Comanche.* He was found by the river with a couple of holes in him and two arrows. No doubt he was in suffering. The cavalry that came to aid Custer was obviously too late. They found him standing down by the river, doctored his wounds, and nourished him back to health, so he could be lead back to Fort Lincoln. The commander at Fort Lincoln said that he will never be ridden again, but they did lead him in parades. He lived well over 20 years past that battle. When he passed away they had him preserved beautifully by a taxidermist standing with his ears forward and a military saddle and bridle on him.

He was standing in a glass cube to help preserve him. While I was standing there looking at him, I was trying to imagine what he went through in that battle. Then we went on to Hudson, Iowa to visit our friends that drove teams in Cheyenne's *Frontier Days* with us. Ron and Kaye Degner, and Dick and Marie Brown, both families had black Percherons that they used in parades in Iowa and they would take them to Cheyenne every July for *Frontier Days.*

Dick sent me with Marie to a parade, after the parade we took the hitch to Waterloo. I was to do the driving for Marie. Dick had another parade to go to with another one of his teams. In Waterloo, we were to go to the museum, and pick up a historian that was to stand up front with me. He was to face the tourists and tell them of the historical places we were passing. I didn't realize all the history in Waterloo,

Iowa. To mention a few: the church where Billy Sunday preached, if you don't recognize the name, he was a preacher like our Billy Graham, only years earlier. The Sullivan brothers' home and the park across the street from their home was where they played as kids. The city has built a large memorial there in remembrance of that family. The Sullivan family had five sons and one daughter. World War II came along and all five sons joined the Navy. The youngest one was the only one married and they requested to be on the same ship together. The Navy agreed. They shipped them to the South Pacific to join the battle with the Japanese. Their ship was sunk and all five sons were lost and are entombed in their ship for all eternity, entombed at the bottom of the ocean. It was very moving to see that memorial. We saw the train station where their father would walk down to catch his train that he was conductor on for years. The navy notified Mr. and Mrs. Sullivan of their loss. The next morning, Mr. Sullivan put on his conductor's uniform and hat, kissed his wife and walked down to the depot and caught his train as he always did. I'm sure that was therapy for him, to go to work the next day. Since then the government initiated the Sullivan Law that brothers can't serve together in the service but today I think that has been repealed. Just another job I really enjoyed, back to Hudson to the Degners for a little more visit. Ron's son was a hog raiser big time. He marketed ten thousand head per year. They were housed in buildings that automatically kept the temperature the same year round. The pigs never touched the ground. They walked on steel grates. Their droppings went through the steel grates that they walked on. Then the droppings were made into slurry pumped into trucks and spread on fields for fertilizer. Their pens had automatic feeders while they were growing and gaining weight. Momma pig is having another litter and on goes the cycle.

While we were there, Ron was taking his weekly load to the slaughterhouse. He loaded up his semi trailer, with a load of pigs, about 225 pounders. We had to get in line at the slaughter house because there were ten semis ahead of us. Iowa is one of the largest pig raising states in our country. It wasn't until we were backed in to unload, that Stan and I got out of the truck. Immediately, they made us put on rubber boots and step into a tank with a disinfectant solution in it. I asked the weigh master, how many hogs a day do they slaughter and he said about 16,000 per day. So my friends get to eatin' bacon. We left Stan and Viv, they were heading east, and we started for home, back through Trenton, Nebraska to see some cousins still living there. We then went to Montrose for a couple of days rest and a good visit with more cousins, and then on to El Centro. It was yet another wonderful trip to see America.

Helping Tim Kirby

My nephew, Tim Kirby was working for the Wolf Cattle Company on the Little Cone Base Camp. It was a satellite ranch up in the high country, 75 miles south of Montrose, Colorado. He was in charge of their cattle up there in the high country for the summer pasture. He was living in a two-story cabin that the company furnished for him during the summer.

He came down to Montrose for supplies one day and I was talking to him about his work. It sounded like what I had been doing for years, so I asked him if I could come up and ride herd with him one day. "Sure.", he replied and he gave me directions on how to find him. I threw my saddle in the back of the pickup, and off I went the next morning early. I followed Tim's directions exactly. Ten miles off the paved road we traveled. Dirt road. Leading up, up, up, all the way up. I arrived at the gate and the sign said "Little Cone Base Camp - Altitude 10,000 feet."

Tim cooked a nice dinner and went to bed for a good night's sleep. We woke up early for a little breakfast, and then saddled up our horses. He gave me a big gray horse to ride. Tim was talking to me while we were saddling up, telling me what we were going to do that day. We mounted up and started up the trail into the timber country. He told me he had about 35 head that had left the herd out in the meadow and had wandered off into the high timber. So we were going to look for them. It took us all day walking through timber searching through the trees with the branches trying to knock us off our horses. Every once in a while we would come to a downed tree and my old gray horse would have to jump over it.

We could hear the steers breaking branches as they were walking ahead of us. After several hours in the saddle, we finally got them rounded up and started home. I never saw a more pretty sight, that cabin off in the distance. I'm sure *old gray* felt the same as I did. We arrived late in the afternoon. I thanked Tim for the opportunity to ride with him. We said our goodbyes, shook hands and a big hug. I got in my pickup and started down the mountain. I arrived home in Montrose after dark. That was a hard day for this old man, especially at a 10,000 foot altitude with thin air, but a good dinner at the Cameo Buffet helped get my energy back. The whole affair left me a great memory of my nephew.

Knotts Berry Farm

In 1996, Marilyn and I were at Knott's Berry Farm having lunch at the Chicken Shack.

I asked Marilyn, "Do you think they would hire an old guy like me to work for the summer months? We could bring the grandkids up to stay with us all summer. One kid at a time, two weeks at a time and take them to Knott's Berry at night for fun. On days off we could go to the beach and also the RV park. Where we are staying has a pool where the kids could play in."

She said, "I saw the human resource office back there, go and see."

We finished our lunch. I went into the human resource office, asked about employment and the girl handed me an application. I filled it out. She told me to be seated and they would give me an oral interview. Soon, they called me in to another office. We met, shook hands, and I begin to tell the interviewer what I was looking for in employment; that was to drive the stage coach ride. I told him my experience with horses and driving teams. He told me that there were no openings on the stage coach at this time, but if I would be willing to work at the gold mine until they had an opening on the stage?

I said, "Sure." They asked me if I could come in Monday and get my uniform and I told him that I'd be there.

"Just tell me where to go and what time." The day that I was to show up, they issued me uniforms. They told me they had made an appointment for me with their doctor for a physical. I did it all on Monday and started panning for gold Tuesday at 11:00 am. I met another miner that was on duty and he gave me some instructions on how to pan for gold and how to use their slush box. I had it down pat in one lesson and from then on I really had fun with the kids panning for gold. I'd watch their eyes light up when they really found gold. We would put the gold they found in a little glass bottle and they would skip off to show their parents.

I was there at the gold mine for the first few working days, and then they sent me to the old jail to talk to people looking through the jail house bars using a hidden microphone. Some people would slip me the name of the person looking at me through the bars. So when I called them by name, they would react in all different ways. Some of them would jump back and say "How does he know my name?" After a few days of the jail house experience, they moved me to relief breaks in the Calico Saloon, Blacksmith Shop, Museum, and Judge Roy Bean's Saloon, which was his courthouse, complete with the big oil painting of Lili Langtree hanging on the wall behind the bar. She was the judge's idol. Compare the old judge's trial costs to our court costs today. Judge Roy Bean's cost to execute a horse thief was $3.00 for a rope and he always bragged that he never hanged an innocent man; and by the way no alcoholic beverages are served in any of the saloons on the grounds of the park. Sarsaparilla, sodas and tea were the strongest beverages served.

One month now had gone by, but at last they came to me and told me I start on the stage coach Monday because of my experience with horses. I was just like a little kid that had just found a sucker. I could hardly wait till Monday morning. They sent me back to wardrobe for my new uniform because I was to stay there for the rest of the summer. I showed up at the barn a little early and just stood there looking around. I noticed on the wall were the names of 52 horses. Four lines of names. I started at the top of the first list and about halfway down the list was a horse named *Jack*. I said to myself, "Oh, that's an omen." I continued on down the list then over the next list of names and down to the fourth name, you will never guess. The horse's name was *Kirby*. *That was a double omen.* That proved to me that I'm supposed to be in this place in the barn working with horses at Knott's Berry Farm. I'm not superstitious, but you explain that.

The boss took me into the harness room and showed me how to hang them by name, showed me the stagecoaches and showed me how we are to lead a horse as if I didn't know how, but I listened to him explain how he wanted it done. He showed me how to harness a horse, how to curry a horse, he showed me where the wash rack was, where sometimes it was necessary to wash a horse. He showed me how they wanted me to unharness a horse, how to carry the harness, and how it is to be hung up. Then they told me just to follow the barn foreman all day for the first day. Watch and learn. They gave me a drawing with a harness on a horse, which each strap and buckles had its name out at the side. They wanted me to memorize each strap and buckle. I think that was the only test I ever took in all of my schooling that I got a 100%.

He had one horse named *Cliff*, that was rank and you didn't know when he was going to explode. Sometimes it was when you put the harness on him or sometimes when you take it off. Sometimes he was calm. I saw him stomp his groomer pretty bad and had to send the kid to the doctor. All the time that I had been there, I never had *Cliff* on my shift. I had to harness twelve to twenty horses a day, clean some stalls once every two weeks.

Finally, I got on the stage coach. One night we were coming back to the barn which was across the street from the park and *Cliff* was on my hitch. They had hooked him up as my right "wheeler" horse all the way back to the barn. It was my job that night to unhook the teams and take the harnesses off.

I was prayin', "Lord, I don't want to unharness that horse, *Cliff*. I don't know how you are going to help me out here, but I need help please, Lord. Take this horse from me." I was still praying when we pulled into the barn. I climbed down off of the stage. I walked up to my lead team, unhooked them, and led them over to the hitching rail and tied them up. I started back to get my wheelers, which included *Cliff*. I unhitched them from the stage, led them to their hitching rail, still praying, and tied them still praying.

I started on my left wheeler and my supervisor walked up and said, "Jack, let me help you. I haven't unharnessed a horse in about eight years."

I quickly said, "Here take this one." and quickly pointed to *Cliff* and he said okay. I bent down behind my horse and said, "Thank you Lord, you always meet my needs. You ain't done nothin' for me, but good." *Cliff* didn't explode and my supervisor didn't get hurt, and I was thankful for that too. I'm just too old to get a bunch of hurt on me anymore. I finished grooming my horses and put them in their pens. A good four hours on the hitch. I got in my car and went home.

Pulling a shift in the blacksmith shop.

The stage coming into the dock to unload.

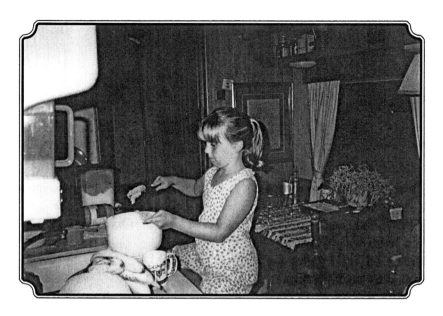

Taryn, our granddaughter, baking banana bread while visiting us at Knott's Berry Farm.

Marsie, our granddaughter, relaxing on Marilyn during her turn to visit us at Knott's Berry Farm.

Buffalo, Oklahoma

Bob Kirby saw an ad in a RV magazine that advertised for a senior couple with an RV to work on the Adams ranch in the summer of 1995. They could park at the ranch in Buffalo, Oklahoma. I mailed off a letter to Mr. Adams, telling him that I had been herding cattle here in Imperial Valley for 24 years and that I would like to come to Buffalo to work for him.

One month went by and we never heard from him. His phone number was on the ad, so I called him. He told me that when he put that ad in the RV travel magazine he had no idea he would get the response that he got. He said, "I have a bushel basket full of mail and I have only read a few of them. Tell me about your letter." So, I told him what I wrote, about me working cattle for 24 years in our Valley. He stopped me right there and said, "Oh, yeah! I remember that one." He then said to me, "Okay, if you want the job, it's okay with me and I'll just burn all these other letters." He told me when to come and how to find the ranch. Marilyn and I packed up the RV and headed east, slowly but surely, enjoying the scenery. We headed to El Paso, Texas and visited my nephew, Tom and his family. We left El Paso and headed for Abilene, Texas to the famous Ranch Rodeo where Stan and Viv were waiting for us; where six huge cattle ranches in Texas and Oklahoma. Each ranch had a team of 6 hands to compete against the team of cowboys from the other ranch. Now, that is pure rodeo and very entertaining. It was all indoors and every seat was excellent, five days of fun, campfires, parades downtown, cowboy poetry and readings, and specialty acts. They brought a Mustang in the arena where they had a small portable arena set up and they let the Mustang loose inside of it. A cowboy they call the Horse Whisperer was going to get on his back within thirty minutes without him swallowing his head and going to buckin'. First thing he had to do was catch him and then put a halter on him. Then he started from there rubbing him all over his body and talking to him very softly. It was something to watch. He had the audience spellbound, and he was on that horse, no buckin' in thirty minutes.

The events and competition were calf roping, team roping, and bronc riding, roping and branding. They would rope a calf, drag him to the fake fire, throw the calf down and hold him down and brand him with white paint and a brush. All the events were timed, except the bronc events. We really enjoyed Abilene, then. Stan, Viv, Marilyn and I had hit the trail for Dallas, and then north heading for Oklahoma City. Stan dropped off before we got there, at a lake and stayed there for a while. There were good catfish fries daily. Marilyn and I went on to Dodge City, Kansas. There's a lot of Old West history in Dodge and we stayed there until we had to leave for old Buffalo.

The next morning we were on our way to Buffalo and a new experience in our lives. We got to town about 11:00AM and took off for the Adams ranch according to the directions Craig Adams had given me. It was east of town, about eight miles, then north seven miles on a dirt road until you came to the feed lot on the right side of the road. We pulled in and found a place to park down by one of the barns that had electricity. We plugged in and waited for Craig to show up. The flies were horrendous and all over the screen door. Marilyn couldn't handle it, so the next morning, we went back to Buffalo. I had seen an RV park that had six hookups, water, electricity and sewer, and no flies. We went down to the Dairy Queen for dinner that night. We got a good night's sleep and I gave Marilyn a good night kiss and assured her everything was going to be fine. The next morning, another kiss and goodbye, *expect me when you see me*, and down the road I went.

I got to the ranch and found Craig waiting for me and got in his pickup and went out over the plains looking for and checking on his windmills to make sure they were pumping and the tanks had plenty of water for the cattle. It was a 35-mile round trip out over the prairie, to check five windmills. Later on, we were back at the ranch. We sat there in the truck and talked. Come to find out, he had 11,000 acres and 3500 head of yearlings. He and some of the other hands were going out to round up some the next day and bring them into the yard. They were going to dehorn and brand them and give them their shots. I told him that was more my thing than windmills, even though I had a windmill on our farm in California. It was the only windmill in the Valley because there wasn't enough wind for two of 'em. So, I asked if I could I go along with them on a horse and he said, sure.

The next morning, when I got out at the ranch he had a horse for me. We loaded 'em up and started out across the plains to a spot where some of the hands had set up a portable corral. We were going to ride out across the prairie, and round up a bunch in that area that needed processing. The cattle trucks were on their way to load, so we got on our horses and started out across the grasslands in search of our cattle. We were on the old Chisholm Trail in Kansas and every hill I came up on, my imagination would let me see John Wayne coming up over the next hill. It was wonderful, just like being home in the saddle again. We found our steers and moved them into the portable corral and loaded them in trucks that had now arrived and were waiting for us. We got 'em all loaded and back to the ranch where we unloaded them and that was all for the day.

Craig wanted me to check the windmills on Mondays, Wednesdays, and Fridays. I took off the next morning to check on them and the water tanks and went back to the ranch to process the cattle we brought in the day before. It had started to rain pretty good now and the other hands were already there and had started working on the steers. I was late, so they put me outside with a whip to keep the steers coming up to the pinch chute.

The pen where the steers were, was now muddy, mixed with manure and they had it splashed all over me, even on my face. My boots and pants' leg were covered with all that gook. We finished the day and went back to town before dark. Marilyn wouldn't let me in the RV like I was. She insisted that I take off all clothes clear down to my shorts and then come in the house. I stuck my boots and clothes under the RV until the next morning, gave a wave to the neighbors, and went in and took a good hot shower. Marilyn had prepared a good hot meal for me. I visited a little with her, told her about my day, told her how much I loved her and thanked her for letting me do this job when I knew it wasn't fun for her. And so it went each week, windmills and cattle.

The last week we were there, all hands were going up to Kansas to round up and ship two truckloads to Liberal, Kansas. We got there on all dirt roads out in that country, well off the paved roads. We were early, before the trucks got there. There was one pickup in front of my pickup, with three cowboys sitting in it talking. I had let my tailgate down and was sitting on it talking to a cowboy standing in front of me with his hands on his hips and his legs sprawled out. I saw a cloud of dust coming down the road that pulled in where we were all parked. This gal got out of a Ford Bronco. She had a cigarette in her mouth and a can of beer in her hand. The cowboy standing in front of me said, "Hello Honey, come over here. I want you to meet Jack Kirby from California. He is working with us on the Adams ranch. Jack, this is my wife." She shook my hand, "It's nice to know you," she said, never taking the cigarette out of her mouth. She then walked up to the cowboys sitting in the other pickup and all of the sudden the air turned blue with some of the worse swearing I had ever heard. I mean it was foul language.

    I turned around to see what was going on, and then I looked back at her husband who was standing in front of me. He had the biggest smile on his face, ear to ear. Looking right at me "Ain't she sweet," he said. I shook my head yes, and laughed. We finished our work and got the cattle loaded and back on our way to Liberal, Kansas. Craig asked me if Marilyn and I would come over to his house the next night for dinner and to meet his wife and kids. We did. He lived in a beautiful home in town. We had a nice meal, visited for a while, said our goodbyes, and thanked Craig for the work. He said I was a good hand and that I could come back next summer if I wanted to. I told him thanks, but I'm always looking for something new. The next day was Sunday, we don't travel Sundays. So we found a little country church, enjoyed the service, then lunch at the Dairy Queen, and then kicked back the rest of the day. The next morning, we headed for Coffeeville, Kansas, where Stan and Viv were waiting for us to see all the history in Coffeeville, another historical old city.

We got 'em all rounded up and on their way to Liberal, Kansas.

On our way to round up some cattle in Kansas on the Chisholm Trail.

So You Wanna Be a Cowboy?

One of the windmills I had to check three times a week out on the prairie in Northern Oklahoma.

Here is one of the hands holding my horse, Poco the Black. There are portable corrals set up in the background.

Tragedy with Kaz

My son, Wesley and his wife Caroline's youngest daughter, Amber lived in Palm Desert, California. She bought a great old thoroughbred horse, broke the best. She got him in Palm Springs, called me to see if I could come and pick him up and keep him at John Taylor's Corral in El Centro. I did, and John said "OK." So off we go for Amber's horse in Palm Desert. We picked her up, and then we all headed to pick up her horse. After we got him loaded in our trailer, we started home to El Centro. Amber was going to come down to El Centro on the weekends to ride, which was a good idea because Marilyn and I would get to see her more often. She came down one weekend, rode him, but didn't feel comfortable on him. He was a big horse. So she gave him to her youngest cousin, our youngest granddaughter, Taylor Mae Martin, who was delighted and made great friends with him right away, and he with her. Sugar cubes and carrots will make a bond every time quickly.

His name was *Casanova*, which she called him *Kaz* for short. He was beautiful gray gilding in his twenties. Taylor was after me every day to take her out there to ride and I did as often as I could, and she developed into an excellent rider in the time she owned him. She was ten years of age. Certain days of the week, she would ride him to the equestrian center about a mile from John's house. There she learned to run the barrels and lope around figure eights, which are excellent procedures to learn your balance on a horse. Across from John's house was about three acres of dirt. She would go over there and gallop around the outside of the field. On the back side, where she thought I couldn't see her, she would turn him loose, wide open and let him run. When she would come back around to where I was watching her, I would scold her for doing that.

"Okay, granddad." But she loved to run and would do it all over again, "the brat." John had to be gone from home for a few weeks and all the horses that were being boarded in his corrals were under the care of Mike Taylor. While his dad was away, I was in the hospital having leg surgery in Palm Springs, so I couldn't check on *Kaz* daily as I always did while I was home. I had just gotten released from the hospital, got home and the phone rang, and it was Mike.

He said, "Jack, there is something wrong with your granddaughter's horse. He won't eat his hay or grain. He just stands there with his head down."

I told him, "Mike, if a horse won't eat, it is because he wants water or he has a twisted gut."

He immediately replied to me, "Oh! That's what it is. I remember now. I took him out of his pen and put him in a different pen and now I remember, I had turned the water off in the new pen I put him in about ten days ago. So, he's been without water for ten days."

We all got in the car and drove out to John's to find him just standing there drinking water from a tub that Mike had just put in his pen since our phone conversation. By the time we got there, he had drunk too much and he lay down immediately and died while we were standing there.

That was a horrible thing for Taylor Mae to see. Her grandmother and I tried to comfort her best we could. It was too bad that she was with us and had to see that happen to her horse that she loved dearly. Lesson learned!

When you are dealing with animals, many times tragedies happen like when they have reached the end of their lives and you have to put them down, it is a real heart breaker. Our little midget horse *Thunder* was kicked in the heart by *Tonka Jr*, died instantly, and *Dusty* lived to be 32 years old and had to be put down. *Jerry* got a liver disease and I had to put him down. *Tom* lived to be 30 and had a heart attack and died with his head in my arms. *Slick* suffered an injury in his front leg and had to be destroyed. *Freckles* suffered a rear injury and was put down. *Bucko* went lame in his left front foot and so I sold him to a guy that wanted him instead of putting him down. We lost three dogs, eight cats, our pet turkey, *Lurkey* that the dogs chewed up, had to be destroyed. *Deadle Duck* died of old age and finally, *Dynamite*, our bantee rooster, passed. Robbie sold her pigs and lamb for breeding. Her goats, *Arnie* and *Barnie* that she raised from babies were past their normal life span, and so we destroyed them. So we all focus on the memories and not the dark days.

Taylor, our granddaughter, riding Kaz at the Broken Spoke Golf Course.

Taylor driving Kaz hitched to our pony wagon.

Our Family Ski Trips

In the 1970's, we would take the family, and sometimes the kids would bring a friend, and we would head out to Big Bear or Mammoth Mountain, up in the high Sierras for several days of skiing. The first time we went to Mammoth, we rented all of our equipment, took ski lessons and got hooked. So, when we got home, we all ordered our own equipment and ski clothes. Now, we were all set to go skiing every month or so.

On one trip, in which the family all went, and we had Britt, our Swedish exchange student with us, and Craig Reichert. Everyone called him, "Colombo", because he had one eye that shot a little different than the other, like Peter Faulk, the star that played Colombo in the mini-series. Craig was a great kid and a tough football player. He played left guard offense and would open up the holes for Wes to run through. He played for the mighty Central Spartans. We all skied, everyday and all day. Then we would crash around the fireplace in our condo to watch TV and eat pizza until we all fell asleep. Craig had been diagnosed with terminal neuroblastoma cancer and was undergoing chemo, which of course was causing his hair to fall out. I remember him sitting on the floor one evening in front of the couch and the girls were pulling pieces of hair out of his head, and he would laugh and the girls would pull more. It was a week between his treatments, so he was feeling good while we were there and we really enjoyed being with him. This trip was in January.

The first week of March, Craig was hospitalized. Robin and I were coming home late one evening from the fair and I felt we should stop by to see him on our way home. Robbie and I walked into his room and he was sitting up in bed with a big smile. A wave and a 'hi' to us. We couldn't believe what we were seeing in him because he had been so sick. He said to Robin, "Come here, Robbie. I need a hug.", then I shook his hand. We had some small talk about our ski trip and football games. He acted like he would be going home in the morning. As we left, Robbie gave him another hug. He then shook my hand, looked me in the eye, and said, "Jack, I'll be free, soon."

I wondered all the way home what he meant by that remark. One hour after we got home, the hospital called and told us that Craig had died. It was then, I knew why I felt why we should go by, and it dawned on me what he meant when he said, *Jack I'll be free, soon.* He knew his end was near. Since this happened, I have been told sometimes dying people have a euphoric experience just before death. That explains what we had seen in Craig that night. In our opinion, Craig Reichert has gone to his heavenly home and is free from pain and tears. What a great kid. All through my book I have told stories of tragedies with our animals of all kinds and I want you to remember that they happen to people, too. So enjoy each other, everyday that God has given you.

This is me on a family ski trip to Mammoth Mountain during a snow storm.

Sailing the West Indies

In 1978, John, Vera, their daughter Cheryl, her husband Eddie Kandal, Marilyn, and I booked a sailing trip to the Caribbean around the East Indies on a four-master sailing ship. We all had our own cabins, complete with bathroom and showers. We would sail at night. They gave us mats to lie on the deck and we would watch the stars and the full moon in September before going to our cabins. The ship would sail into a cove at some island and drop anchor. We would then swim to shore or order a water taxi. The water was crystal clear. You could see fish, rocks, and sand. The bottom was at least 100 feet deep.

While anchored, if we didn't want to go to shore we would tie a rope to a yard arm and swing out over the water and drop in. It was a lot of fun. We flew into Puerto Rico, spent the night then caught a flight on an old DC-3 that had a bad oil leak in one engine. We flew to St. Thomas where we would catch our sailing ship. We were met on board with a Caribbean band that played and we danced half the night away. On our return flight, I suggested to stop off in New Orleans for a couple of days and enjoy some oysters. I had a special place that I knew. We did and we really enjoyed ourselves. Then, on home to get ready for the fall cattle season, which was about the first of October.

This is the Four Master that we sailed the West Indies on in the Caribbean Sea.

Flying: Another New Experience

My adult Sunday school teacher had been a flight instructor in World War II in the Army Air Corps, but was now retired. One Sunday after class, he told me that he had found a Luscombe-AE all-metal airplane for sale in Yuma, AZ. He told me if I would buy it, he would give my brother Stan and I flight instructions until we could get our pilot's license at no charge as long as I would let him fly it whenever he wanted to. I quickly agreed, so my friend, Joe Hooker and I left for Yuma the next morning. I bought the plane and Joe flew it back to the airport in Imperial. We made arrangements to tie it down there. Then Stan and I patiently waited for our first lesson.

After eight hours of dual flight, landings and take-offs and after shooting several landings, Joe had me taxi back to the end of the runway. He got out of the plane and told me to take off and land two times, just touch and go alone. He would stand there and watch. Both Stan and I did as he said and we did very well, with a little extra sweat on our foreheads, I might add. Joe then helped us plan a three-hour solo cross-country flight. Now, in the early 50's, to get a pilot's license, all you needed was eight hours of dual flight with an instructor and three hours of solo cross-country and then you qualified for your license. My next flight, I flew my cross-country, a three-hour flight. The next day, we called the FAA for our test flights and we both passed.

In 1951, it was very easy to get a pilot's license and it wasn't long before I wanted a larger four-passenger plane. I sold the Luscombe and bought a Stinson Voyager, just like the one in the picture, same color and all. Stan and our wives flew together a lot and we really enjoyed that part of our lives. Marilyn in 1955 said to me, "Jack, you have babies coming and lots of responsibility." and that I should sell the plane, and of course, she was right. That ended five years of lots of fun in the air.

I got my first air plane in 1950. It was an all-metal Luscombe.

In 1951, I traded in my first plane for a Stinson Voyager.

Mexico City Olympics

Two years before I sold my company, Kirby Foods in 1967, my brother Stan and I partnered up and acquired an old established distributing company in Indio, California. Stan and his wife Vivian moved to Indio and bought a nice home. They took over the management of our newly acquired company that was top heavy in agriculture supplies. They also sold janitorial merchandise.

An elderly couple that was tired and had lost interest owned this old company. They were suffering many losses in the agriculture supply end of it because the farmers had a few bad financial losses, for a few years in a row. The farmers were unable to pay their bills in full, which had a domino effect, causing their company unable to pay their bills. We took it on with the contingency that we could straighten it out in a few years or give it back. Therefore, off we go on a new experience in our young lives.

I was already servicing that area out of my El Centro plant. We also decided to add groceries to our inventory in Indio. I handed all my accounts over to Stan. Sales volume began to grow. My El Centro plant did all of the manufacturing, packing and shipping of the products that were not large enough to purchase directly from suppliers.

In 1968, Stan, Vivian, Stan's secretary Rita Lopez, Rita's husband Zeke, Marilyn, and myself, ordered tickets to the 1968 Olympics in Mexico City to 19 different events.

We all took separate flights and separate hotels, because that is all we could schedule. Marilyn and I flew out of Mexicali, directly to Mexico City. We arrived first. My plant manager at the time, whose name was Oscar Castillo, who was a wonderful young employee, had his uncle meet us at the airport and take us to our hotel. We gathered our luggage and off we went to our hotel. It was not what we expected or what we wanted, so our new found friend agreed we should not stay in that hotel. He told us that he would take us to an excellent hotel that he knew was very good. He pulled up in front of the Golden Suite Hotel, downtown. Our suite was on the third floor. It had 2 bedrooms, a kitchen, bathroom, and living room with a great view that looked out over the city. The glass window was from the top of the ceiling to the floor, and wall to wall. What a wonderful sight, especially at night.

Oscar's uncle went back to the airport to pick up Stan and Vivian when their flight landed. He brought them directly to the Golden Suite Hotel. Zeke and Rita, knowing their way around Mexico City, went directly to their hotel. We knew where they were staying, so we met them for breakfast at their hotel, which was a converted convent with four sides, and a flower garden to enjoy and eat your meals there. I told them at breakfast that morning, that on the flight down, I was reading a magazine that I found on the plane, about a restaurant built around a small bullring. Dining tables and chairs were where the audience would sit for a real bullfight and have dinner while watching whoever was fighting the bull. Eat and holler "Olé" when the bull makes his passes. The article said that anyone that wanted to try making a few passes with a bull could, for a charge of $20. The restaurant was located about 10 miles north of the city. All the way to the Café and bullring, I kept saying, "I'm going to fight a bull, but I don't want a cape or a sword. I just want man against beast." However, the closer I got to the ring, the more nervous I was getting. I had been shooting off my mouth about "man against beast." I couldn't wait to get there—I had to go to the bathroom, and the closer we got, the more I had to go.

Just before we arrived, we crossed a bridge. I looked down at the small river. Mexican women were on their knees pounding their clothes on the rocks that they had just washed in the river. In the background was a view of high-rise buildings on the skyline of a modern city. It was unbelievable. I wouldn't have believed it if I hadn't seen it for myself.

We drove into the parking lot of the bullring and restaurant and went it. I quickly located the men's restroom and got that out of the way. We all found our table for dinner—it was overlooking the bullring. I immediately began to back track and say I was just kidding, but the gang wouldn't let up. So I went down to meet my adversary. I met the instructing matador, and after a few minutes of instruction, he took me out on the catwalk. Below the catwalk, there were pens full of bulls in every size; they started out small and progressed to adult, fighting bulls. They would sometimes have a matador visiting for dinner, and they would ask him to make a few passes for the crowds of folks having dinner.

I found a bull I thought I could handle. His horns were about five inches long and just beginning to turn forward. The matador told me he was about 500 pounds, so that's the one I chose. We went back to the dressing room, and I paid him the twenty dollar charge. He then showed me an alter with candles and a crucifix with a kneeling rail in front of it. He said I could pray if I wanted to, and I wanted to... really bad.

He handed me a pair of heavy leather pants, which I put on over my trousers. Then he gave me a leather hat and handed me the cape, which he had already shown me how to use. I was taught to move aside when the bull charged, and let him hit the cape.

Over the loud speaker came an announcement. "Ladies and gentlemen: Señor Jack Kirby is going to be performing as our evening matador." The bull fighting music began, and the doors opened up to "The Ring." I put the cape over my shoulder and walked very proudly with my lower lip stuck out. I walked across the ring to where Marilyn was seated, and I threw her my hat. She waved it and threw it back. I moved out to the center of the ring holding my cape and bracing myself for what was about to happen.

"No cape--just man against beast." Why did I say that? Why! Why! Why! What in the world had I gotten myself into? I told the matador to release the bull. Keep in mind that these animals are bred to be mean from birth, which I didn't know at the time. The gate flew open and the beast came toward me on a dead run. I froze in place. I immediately forgot what the matador had told me, so I prepared for a collision. I gritted my teeth, closed my eyes, and took the bow on my thighs. The next thing I knew, I was turning a flip in the air. My back landed on the ground, and the beast was trying to gore me with his horns.

The matador came to my rescue with his cape and got the bull's attention. I scrambled to my feet, and out of the ring I went. The matador said, "No, no, no Señor. "You must step aside and let the bull hit the cape. Not you, Señor."

So I gave it another try. I walked back in the ring, took my matador position, and hollered, "A-ha, Toro!" That got his attention, and he came back towards me to finish me off. I made a successful pass this time. The more the bull hit the cape, the crowd would say, "Olé!" When I finally had enough, they turned the beast out. I took my bows and walked around the ring with my hat in my hand. I threw kisses to my newfound friends who were applauding and hollering, "Olé!" I strutted out of the ring as if I had just conquered the world. The matador gave me a large, colored poster of a matador and a bull with my name and date at the bottom.

I often think about that experience and wished I had read Ernest Hemmingway's book, *Death in the Afternoon*, before stepping into the ring. However, had I read the book, I would have probably never had this adventure.

We went on to enjoy all 19 events that we had tickets for and visited many sites in the city. At the end of our two weeks in Mexico City, we all said our goodbyes, got in our separate air planes, and flew off for home.

Nebraska: My Home State

One year after *Frontier Days*, we went to North Platte, Nebraska and did the grand entry for the rodeo with *Tom* and *Jerry*. Then we went on down to Trenton, Nebraska for their *Pow Wow Days Parade*, a big cowboy dance and rodeo. The rodeo always has an event called 'barrel racing.' The girls on their fast, quick quarter horses, would run around three barrels as fast as they could go in a figure-eight pattern. After the last girl would go on her run, we would arrange with the announcer to say, "Wait a moment folks, we have a late entry.", and Robin would come in on big *Jerry* running as fast as he could and go around the barrels. The quarter horses would clock about sixteen seconds and big *Jerry's* time was always about 65 seconds or more. The crowd would applaud and laugh and they really enjoyed it. Robbie did it every year at different rodeos and if she wasn't with us, we would draft a clown to do it also.

Now, the *Pow-Wow* was held at Trenton where the last war between Indian tribes in our nation took place. The Pawnee and the Sioux tribes would take part in the celebration. The two tribes would meet at a sacred ground area, north of town. They would have a fire ring scene and beat their drums and dance. Then one Indian would stand in the middle of the circle and say something in Indian and then shoot an arrow to the north, one to the east, one to the south, and another to the west. Everyone there for the ceremony was told not to look for the arrows; nor were they to disturb the arrows where they had landed. It was in memory of what happened there on that spot and was done in the memory of the dead warriors of both tribes. It was very interesting to see.

The parade was three blocks long so we and all those in the parade would go the three blocks, then turn around and go back through again. We were first, the first time through and last, the second time through. Mom was the grand marshal because she was born in Trenton. Actually she was born in a two-room stone house nine miles north of Trenton that her dad had built out on the plains. I was born one mile farther down that dirt road. After the parade, mom wanted to take *Tom* and *Jerry* up to the old folk's home and show them the team. We called the management and told them that we were coming so they brought out all the patients that were mobile outside of the home and lined them all, up close to the team. One elderly lady that I will never forget was 85 years old and blind. She walked up to *Jerry* with an assistant and she asked me if she could touch him. I told her, of course she could. So her caregiver put her hand on *Jerry's* head, then she made her hand go down his neck slowly and the tears began to flow down her wrinkled cheeks. Then her hand went down across his back, slowly around his rump, and the tears kept coming. By now, she had us all teary. It was very quiet for all who was there watching her. *Jerry* was so patient and didn't move a muscle. It was an experience for that dear lady. She was brought to me and she said, "Thank you, sir, for allowing me that wonderful experience." The tears were still streaming down her cheeks. She said it brought back many, many memories when her father farmed the plains of Nebraska with horses. *Bless her heart.* We were so thankful we could brighten her day, just a little. We wished them all well as they went back into the home. My mom was so thankful that she had come along with us to Trenton where she still knew so many folks, even some of those in the rest home.

After the visit, mom wanted me to take her out to the old stone house where she was born in 1904. That is still standing out on the prairie. Her granddad came out to Nebraska driving a team and wagon in 1864 from Iowa. Our family history said my great granddad Smith got held up for two days in Nebraska to let a herd of buffalo pass. The buffalo moved so slow, grazing prairie grass and just moseying along. After they passed, they broke camp, harnessed the team, and continued on their way to southwestern Nebraska to Homestead, where there was 160 acres that the government offered to anyone who wanted to go out west.

He found what he wanted when he got to a little settlement on the Republican River. The people there called it Trenton. The acreage that he found was about nine miles north of Trenton. He wanted to be near a town of some kind for groceries and supplies, so he staked out his claim and found a hill where he could dig out a cave and call it home. He finally made the dugout big enough so that he and great grandma could live in it. They unloaded the wagon and moved in. After one year of living there, he was finally able to build a small house to start their family. By 1901, my mom's dad married Martha Miller. Granddad Guy went down Bovey Canyon and built the two-room stone house from stones he picked up from the ground and loaded it in his wagon. He took them to a clearing that he had picked with a big tree on it and this was where he wanted to build his house. I brought two stones home with me taken from the partially crumbled wall and placed them in my front yard; a little bit of my mom's history is still with me.

Now, one room was the kitchen and dining area and living room. The other room was the bedroom. Both rooms were the same size, eight foot by ten foot. Of course, an old out house was built about fifty feet from the house. Can you imagine going out there in the dark during a snow storm? Granddad bought some calves he raised for meat and to sell as well as a milk cow, of course. He had a team that he could farm with or ride to town, so he would take the wagon with a couple of horses hooked up to go for supplies.

My mom was born in that little stone house on the prairie in 1904. Granddad Guy finally was able to build a house one mile further down the trail in 1917. My mom married my dad in 1922 at the age of 17 and moved to town. My dad drove a horse-drawn ice wagon for home delivery. He would drive his team before dawn to Stratton, the next town west, about six miles to get ice at their ice house and then back to Trenton to deliver his ice house to house. Then dad would later go to work on granddad's farm.

All of mom's siblings were born on that farm. Mom was the only one born in the stone house. She had three brothers and one sister. The oldest was mom, then Wyatt, Harlan, Ruby and Orin. All attended a little one-room schoolhouse down the road about two miles and it is still standing today. One year, Stan and his family were traveling together and went to the school house to see it. Hanging on the wall was the big clock with the pendulum still hanging on it. The school had been closed for over sixty years. Can you believe that they would close that building but leave that school regulator clock hanging on the wall? You can only guess where that clock is today. My oldest brother, Tom was born in Trenton in 1923, Roger was born in Iowa in 1925, Stan in 1927, and then the Great Depression hit and dad lost his job at Deckors Hog Slaughterhouse in Mason City. He went back to the farm in Nebraska. My folks didn't have any place to stay so they moved in with Granddad Guy in 1930 when I hit the ground.

In 1936 we moved to San Diego. My Uncle Stan Potter was in the food manufacturing and distribution business and hired my dad and gave him a route in Imperial Valley. That lasted until the war came in 1941. My uncle could sell everything that he could manufacture in the San Diego market, especially with the Navy being there. So, he closed the Valley route and that's how we got to El Centro. We have been here ever since.

In Iowa, my family was free Methodist, but El Centro did not have a Free Methodist church, so we started attending the Nazarene Church in El Centro. Their doctrine is basically the same and we have been going there ever since, sitting in the same pew for 74 years. In 1938, my sister, Norma was born in El Centro at the old hospital at 10th and Holt. You can tell by this story, that I have a lot of horsey country in my blood. My mom outlived all of her siblings. Mom passed at 103 years of age. You had to be tough to live like she did during those early years out on the plains.

Then off we went to Colorado Springs for the next parade and rodeo. It was another great time with the hitch. One afternoon, an all-girl riding group from Arkansas had come to Colorado Springs with a rodeo to entertain. They were all about 14 years old and that afternoon, they were doing their riding routine. They were very skilled. During a routine, they were doing the cross-through where they would go through every other horse. Somehow, they happened to get out of sync and one young girl ran into the horse coming next and it knocked her horse over. They were riding close to the arena wall where there was an iron stake holding up a fence. When she was knocked over her head fell on that stake and she was killed instantly. What a horrible thing to happen in front of a crowd. Especially with her parents there watching that tragedy. The next day the girls performed the same procedure in memory of the girl that was killed, but instead of galloping through the routine, they all walked their horses throughout the routine with their heads bowed. There was not a sound in the stand. It was very moving and after, you could hear crying from all over the crowd. They next day we loaded up and headed for Montrose and the Cameo Buffet for a good dinner.

Afterword

We continued to be very close with John and Vera. Sadly, we lost Vera on July 6, 1994. John and I still saw each other on a regular basis. We would go to football games and other events together until he moved to Salinas, California. John is now in a rest home with Alzheimer's. *God bless him.*

It wasn't long before I sold *Slick* because he had gone lame in his front feet. Shortly after this, we decided to downsize our lives. We sold our farm and had an auction inside the house and barn. People came in and they could see how we used our antiques and everything sold except our bed. About halfway into the auction, Marilyn's emotions couldn't handle it any longer, so she left and went to town. When she returned everything was gone, even our oil paintings that we had bought in Europe were gone. We both sat down on the carpet, held each other tight and just cried. We sold the Cameo, sold the golf course, and bought a small mobile home on the first tee box, which is where we still live today.

I told myself that I had to get busy doing something with what's left of me. I wasn't going to sit down in a rocking chair, and in about six months, start rocking. So Marilyn and I saw the world. We have been in every state of the union with the exception of Alaska (the mosquitoes are too big to go there), all over Europe twice, Hawaii twice, Canada, Puerto Rico, the West Indies, and Mexico. We've been to Mazatlan parasailing (try that sometime) as well as Mexico City for the '68 Olympic games. We've also been to the Olympics in L.A., two world fairs, and now we are studying for our finals. We still go golfing a little, fishing in Oregon, and going to a lot of county fairs. We only have four PGA golf tournaments left that we do now: the Bob Hope Classic, the LA Open, the Lake Tahoe/Reno Open, and the San Jose California. That's just enough at this age.

I'm 81 now, and in excellent health. I still don't take any medications. I thank God for a wonderful life and so many memories, and I also thank God for a wonderful wife of 59 years. Yup, she rode those dirty, dusty trails with me for more than a quarter century, good and bad, and still going strong. The Lord has blessed Marilyn and me with such a great life, with three kids, nine grandkids, six great-grandkids, and very good health.

Our bucket list is almost full, but we're looking forward to our final journey. Make sure that you enjoy your life, friends, and family, and also build on your faith. Regardless of what's going on in your life, Romans 8:28 says all things work together for good, for those who love the Lord. Always wear a smile and have a good sense of humor. God bless you.

Appendix

The Crew

John Taylor, "The Boss" .... Professional Wrangler

Jack Kirby .... Retired Businessman

Vera Taylor .... John's Wife

Marilyn Kirby .... Jack's Wife

Maurice Walker .... Professional Ranch Hand

Roy Smith .... Pastor of the Nazarene Church

Gerry Aulis .... Retired Pastor

Burl Wardrup .... Retired Businessman

Benny Derrick .... Retired School Bus Driver

Occasional Hands and Visitors

Wes Kirby	Charlene Wardrup
Robin Kirby	Gwen McGuire
Bob Kirby	Cheryl Taylor
Steve Kirby	Kenna Taylor
Harry Barnum	Mike Taylor
Craig Reichert	Steve Scaroni

Earl Bowler   Jim McDaniel

Kenny Dukes   Orin Smith

Susie Switzer   Pia Carlson*

Johnny Johnson   Britt Swenson*

Ricky Johnson   Dale Mills

Wyatt Smith

* Swedish Foreign Exchange Students

Professional Cattle People that Would Help When Needed

John Kubler   Leland Raley

Stan Switzer   Butch Burch

Jim Galbreath   Wayne Medlin

Tink Johnson   Dickie Johnson

Art Fann

There were always people who wanted to live their dream and go on a cattle drive, but we didn't have enough horses for everyone.

Parades with Tom and Jerry

Palm Springs Western Days

Las Vegas Heldorado Days

El Centro Christmas Parade

Brawley Cattle Call

Calexico Christmas Parade

Holtville Carrot Festival

Boulevard Rabbit Festival

Imperial Fair Parade

Indio Date Festival Parade

Blythe Fair Parade

Niland Tomato Festival

Yuma Silver Spur Parade

Mother Goose Parade (San Diego, CA)

Durango, Colorado

Ouray, Colorado

Montrose, Colorado

Hotchkiss, Colorado

Gunnison, Colorado

Grand Junction, Colorado

Cheyenne Frontier Days, Wyoming

North Platte, Nebraska

Trenton, Nebraska

Colorado Springs, Colorado

Capistrano California Swallows Return Festival

Many Weddings

Funeral

School Activities

During Halftime at Football Games as Spartacus in a Chariot

Celebrities in the Wagon

Bob Hope	Paul Burke
Claude Akins	Annabell Alvarez
Denver Pyle	John Finn
Norma Zimmer	Dee Pickett
Jack Barry	Jimmie Rodgers
Chuck Connors	Santa Claus
Seniors From Rest Homes	Several Legislators and Pro Athletes

About the Author and His Testimony

Jack was born in 1930 out on the prairie of southwest Nebraska about nine miles North of Trenton. Trenton had a population of 726 people. Being that there was no doctor, his mom's cousin and an Osteopath who lived in Trenton delivered him.

He was born with Club Feet. The Osteopath advised his parents to take him to the University of Iowa Clinic and Hospital. He was in and out of that hospital every year for the next six years of his life. They would wrench and cast his feet for the next five years. In 1936, they finally decided on surgery after which both feet and legs were cast up to his groin for six weeks. When the final casts were removed, he was then put into metal leg braces and had to have lots of massaging of his feet and calves from his mom over the next few years. Bless her heart for hours and hours of her labor of love. Jack and his family left Iowa for California in late 1936. After arriving in El Centro, his parents found and joined the Nazarene Church, where his family still attends after 76 years. They still sit in the same pew with his family. Jack and Marilyn were married in this church in 1952. They have three children, nine grandchildren, and six great-grandchildren. They were gloriously saved in a revival with B. H. Wooton at 12:00 p.m. on a Sunday afternoon on January 17, 1954. Besides serving on the church board for forty years, he also served as the Sunday School Superintendent, Church Treasurer, Sunday School Teacher, Song Leader, Youth Leader, and several other positions when necessary.

Jack started his food distributing company in 1949 when he saw an opportunity and a need to supply food to restaurants and school cafeterias. He bought a 1949 Studebaker truck and a handful of groceries in San Diego with no money, only a handshake and a promise that he would pay. That was his first miracle in his business adventures. His fledgling company grew extremely fast. He rented a single-car garage for a warehouse, soon having to move to a four-car garage and then finally to a larger building. In 1955, a dear friend of his, Mr. Roy Womack whose wife was his Sunday school teacher as a teen, was going to tear down a very large two-story building on his property. Jack asked him if he could find someone to move it, would he sell it to him. He quickly said, "Give me one dollar to make it legal, and the building is yours." This was miracle number two. He soon found a company that would move the building for him. They quoted him $3,000 and that it would take approximately a week to get it done. That was miracle number three. A week later he had a two-story building sitting on his property that he had purchased a year earlier. After moving the building, the mover handed him a bill for $1,500. He asked him why it was only half of what the original quote was. His response was, "Jack, because I have taken a liking to you this week just being around you." This was miracle number four.

In that big building he had plenty of room, so he set up a manufacturing department. They began to manufacture mayonnaise, barbeque sauce, french dressing, fountain syrups, bleach, and pot and pan soap. In 1967, a National company was buying up small companies all across the nation. Continental Food Service, with their general offices in Chicago, made him an offer he couldn't refuse. He elected to take a ten year pay off and hired him back to oversee as Vice President of Southern California Division with all the free time he wanted to pursue other things...miracle number five.

While herding cattle with John Taylor and his wife Vera, they were able to win them to the Lord. They were in church every Sunday with their three kids and he was their kids Sunday school teacher.

Over the years they became acquainted with Dr. Gunstream, the Nazarene District Superintendent of the New Mexico district where his brother, Stan was Pastoring. They made a large contribution to their Camp Meeting. The D.S. said to them, "Jack, I am going to pray that God will just back a big truck full of blessings to the edge of a big white cloud and dump the whole load of blessings on you and your family throughout all of your lives." And, that is exactly what happened, and they are still falling on them today.

Jack and Marilyn built a restaurant in El Centro, CA and one in Montrose, CO. They hired two Christian Managers to run them for the next twenty three years. Now, Jack was able to pursue his boyhood dream to become a cowboy. So, for the next twenty four years, he and Marilyn did exactly that. All of the cattle drives, wrecks, stampedes and the showing of their Clydesdale Hitch across the South Western States certainly qualify them to write this book. You will read about the experiences they shared with Christian Cowboys, Preachers and their wives that would help them. While all of this was going on in their lives, Jack still found time to serve four years on the Board of Associates at Pasadena Nazarene College; eight years on the City Chamber of Commerce; eight years on the Salvation Army Board; twenty five years as a Gideon and was an active member of the El Centro Kiwanis Club for thirty two years. In 1985 he built the Broken Spoke Golf Course in El Centro and later sold the Golf Course to his son, Wes.

Hopefully, their book and life stories will be a blessing to those who read it. Follow your dreams and let the Lord lead you in everything you do.

Local Information

Feed lot cattle and pasture cattle were the number one industry in the Imperial Valley. 800,000 head were fattened per year in the eighties. Even though there are no more pasture cattle, that number hasn't changed that much, if any. All our cattle in the Valley now are Holstein calves and they won't gain on pasture. The cattle we used to put on pasture were called "crossbreeds". They were crossed between Brahma, Hereford, Angus and even some Holstein mixed in. The Brahma part can handle the heat that we have here in the Imperial Valley. A Brahma can lie down in the sun and gain weight. That is not so with pure breed Angus or heifers. We have so many dairies now in Southern California that are producing so many Holstein calves that the feed lots are full of them. There was no longer a need to bring in cross breeds from Texas and Oklahoma, so Johnny Taylor yielded to the changing times and retired.

You probably noticed that we had professional wranglers like John Taylor to help us out when we needed extra help. They were always willing to do that when needed it, and those hands would call us when they needed help and John would take his crew and help them out, all free *gratis*. We all knew each other very well and were all good friends. You probably have been wondering how we could move so many cattle out on the roads and highways legally. The reason is that cattle still have the right of way on California roads and four-lane highways with proper traffic control like the CHP.

I forgot to tell a story about where my golf course is today. The Jackson Family had 180 acres of wheat that didn't come up very well, so it wasn't worth harvesting for them. John had his fencing crew fence off all 180 acres and we turned 500 head in to pasture it off. Now 180 acres of normal pasture would last a herd that size six weeks or more, but since it was a poor crop, we had to move them off in less than a week. Little did I know or even think, that I would build a golf course on 60acres of that 180.

The golf course was surrounded on all four sides by John Ryerson's RV and Mobile Home Park. The ground was so salty, it's a wonder how we ever got a blade of grass to come up, but with lots of love and care, and sprinkling with water it is beautiful today. Every Thanksgiving, starting with the first Thanksgiving before we even opened in 1985, our family and friends played nine holes Thanksgiving morning. So now every Thanksgiving morning we have a tournament that my kids named the "Jack Kirby Classic Turkey Shoot", where all prizes given to the winners in certain categories were given a turkey. It is a nine hole contest, a fund-raiser for our high school golf teams. All income goes to the schools. This is our twenty-sixth year, annual tournament. No doubt some day, it will be a memorial tournament. We have had people come from as far as San Diego and Los Angeles.

CPSIA information can be obtained at www.ICGtesting.com
Printed in the USA
LVOW08s1536231013
358274LV00003B/809/P